M000207203

Keeping the Church Relevant

By Breaking the Cycle of Redundancy

By Larry Pyle

With Steve Pyle

Foreword by Dr. Alton Garrison

Other works by Larry Pyle

Stop GOING to Church...The Dynamics of BEING the Church.
Christian Life Publishers, Columbus, GA, 2000

Keeping the Church Relevant By Breaking the Cycle of Redundancy
by Larry Pyle

Copyright © 2013 By Larry Pyle
ISBN-13: 978-0615848563
ISBN-10: 0615848567

Produced under the auspices of Successful Living Concepts, Inc.
3384 Crow Mountain Road, Russellville, AR 72802

Names of some individuals in this book have been changed to protect their identities. Scriptural references have been taken from various translations of the Holy Bible and are referenced accordingly. The books and authors referenced in this book do not constitute their agreement nor support of the contents of this book.

Scripture quotations marked The Message are taken from *The Message: The Bible in Contemporary language,* Copyright by Eugene H. Peterson 1993, 1994, 1995, 1996, 2000, 2001, 2002. All rights reserved.

To contact the author: larrypfs@gmail.com

www.slcinc.org

CONTENTS

Acknowledgments

- **To** Georgiann, my faithful companion, lover, best friend and co-worker for more than four decades;
- **To** the late prophet, friend and counselor, David Wilkerson, who encouraged me to keep going when I wanted to quit;
- **To** Steve Sjogren, who not only taught us how to show the love of Jesus in a practical way, but has been a constant source of encouragement and inspiration through the years;
- **To** my friend and counselor, Ray Beeson for your ongoing critiques, editorial and spiritual guidance;
- **To** my friend and editorial assistant, Jeanne Saul for your patient assistance and encouragement;
- **To** Gary and Pam Babineaux for the hideaway for prayer and writing;
- **To** Perry and Polly Cowin for your love, prayer, and encouragement over the past thirty years and for helping me touch Romania with *Stop GOING to Church*.
- **To** the greatest children any parents could ever have: Chris, Steve and Aimee…Thanks for your love and dedication to Christ, Georgiann and me.
- **And** finally and foremost, to my wonderful Friend, Lord and Savior, Jesus Christ for your Agape!

FOREWORD

There is a familiar statement popularized by its frequent use as a refrigerator poster: "You will know the truth and the truth shall set you free. But first it will make you miserable."

In his new book, Larry Pyle is not necessarily tender but truthfully challenges all of us to consider the price of progress. The price may seem high; but if we are willing to renounce our commitment to redundancy and take "salt and light" outside the walls of the church building, the results just may astound us. If our preferences are so strong we cannot imagine getting out of our comfort zone, we may never realize true revival. While our intentions may have seemed correct, the most spiritually needy may never know of the transforming power of Christ because we never connected with them.

"Every day that we resist necessary change closes a door of opportunity somewhere in the future" (J. Russell Crabtree, The Fly in the Ointment, New York: Church Publishing, Inc., 2008, p. 7).

While some may think this book is only for church leaders, I think every person is called to "make disciples" and can benefit from the challenges Larry gives. This is not just a book of theory or untested principles. Because of our friendship, I am personally acquainted with the experiences he writes about and the ministry journey he and Georgiann have traveled. As I read the manuscript, I chuckled at times; had tears in my eyes occasionally; and yes, even once or twice thought, "He didn't just say that, did he?"

The part of the book that is probably the most necessary for this generation is where he explains the succession plan between him and his son, Steve. "Passing the baton" of leadership and ministry is not easily done and is often not successful. It is imperative that every church concerned about its future read their story. Larry tells about the risk of stepping aside as lead pastor, and Steve shares principles every leadership team needs to know.

If you want to maximize the spiritual impact of your ministry and ensure the effectiveness and longevity of a missional vision, this book is for you.

Alton Garrison, *Assistant General Superintendent of the Assemblies of God.*

PREFACE

My first book was titled, *Stop GOING to Church...The Dynamics of BEING the Church*. While searching for a title for this new book I was tempted to title it, *No Really, Stop Just GOING To Church and start BEING the Church!* But, reason won out and I resisted the temptation of a cheap commercial for the first book.

Although the message of this book can be vital to the life of any organization, the primary focus is to challenge the thinking and the actions of church leaders. With that in mind I begin by presenting some probing questions: What personal price are you willing to pay to move forward? Are you willing to sacrifice YOUR methods for THE mission? Have you reached a place where your personal comfort is more valuable than the development and success of others? Has your organization reached a place of stagnation and plateau? If so, what changes are you willing to make to generate new life for yourself, your team, and those you serve?

After serving more than thirty years in the role of senior pastor in both denominational and non-denominational circles, I have witnessed and experienced the pain of change and the price of progress. As a result of my journey I have concluded that the continued survival and progress of any organization is contingent upon the willingness of its leaders to make the difficult decisions necessary to perpetuate forward motion. Remember, retirement is not an option for leaders, and we all are *gressing*! The question I will pose for you in the following pages is "How are you gressing?" Are you Digressing, Regressing or Progressing? If you are a Christian leader and desire to follow God's plan, there is only one choice.

INTRODUCTION

We all live in a state of constant change. From our physical bodies to the natural world around us, we are ever experiencing change. We witness it in the educational field, where the training of our children has moved from the home to one-room schoolhouses, to vast campuses where masses of young minds are challenged by ultra-modern technology and ultra-liberal worldviews.

We have witnessed vast changes in our economic system. Where once our currency was backed by solid gold, we now transact business with strips of paper called promissory notes so devalued that the worth of our dollar today is worth only a fraction of what it was twenty five years ago. And where once debt was considered to be a curse, it has now become a norm that threatens the very existence of our nation as a world leader.

We have also witnessed major changes in the Church. As I read the Bible, it seems clear the Church today holds slight resemblance to the early Church. The explosion of technology in our world has led many to alter the methods of presenting the Gospel. The microwave, fast-food, instant-messaging, technocratic, and A.D.D. generation we now live in seems incapable of, or unwilling to tolerate the previous methodology.

We will examine a number of these changes and allow you, the reader, to determine which constitutes progress. For we know things are not always as they appear. And, according to the words of Jesus Christ, principles of the Kingdom of God often run counter to those of the earthly kingdom. For instance, Jesus proclaimed that "Anyone who loses His life for my sake will gain it; Give and you will receive; He who desires to be exalted should humble himself;" and "The last shall be first and the first shall be last."

Strangely, many of us who profess to be Christian believers seem willing to accept change in every area of life except the Church. We know change is inevitable in our physical bodies, in the weather around us, in the political realms and cultural modalities that surround us. But, to embrace changes in the way we do church almost appears sacrilegious to many. However, to ignore change is to embrace redundancy, and to accept redundancy is to embrace death.

Throughout this book, I will distinguish between the true Church of Jesus Christ with a upper case "C" and man's church with a lower case. Additionally, I will refer to the devil with a lower case "d."

Chapter One

The Curse of Redundancy

Oscar Wilde once said, *"I simply hate, detest, loathe, despise, and abhor redundancy."*

Webster's dictionary defines redundancy as "exceeding what is necessary or natural; needlessly repetitive." Redundancy is a cancer that slowly but surely drains the life out of any organization, usually without anyone recognizing a problem until it is too late. Redundancy in the workplace turns creativity and productivity into boredom and mediocrity. But, nowhere is redundancy more critical and more deadly than in the Church of the Lord, Jesus Christ.

A short distance from the famous Westminster Abby in London a sign was posted that read "Advisory Board for Redundant Churches." What? An advisory board for what? The very phrase should be an anomaly to any individual who understands the origin, the character and the definition of the Church. The true Church, the true Body of Christ, by nature and by design, can never become redundant, or it ceases to be the Church and simply becomes a "church."

In my previous book *Stop Going to Church, the Dynamics of Being the Church,* I defined and described the Church according the Word of God. A close look at the Church that Christ established reveals that His Church defies redundancy. Yet, around the world, institutions that once beamed the light of the Gospel, have become lifeless carcasses, with little, if any semblance of their former stature and purpose. Nowhere is that more evident than in Europe, where grand exhibitions of architecture project death and darkness instead of life and light.

There, buildings that once housed Bible-believing congregants, have been, and are now being transformed into museums, theaters, restaurants, pubs, mosques, and Sikh temples. Overall, at least 10,000 churches have been closed in Britain since 1960, including 8,000 Methodist churches and 1,700 Anglican churches. Another 4,000 churches are set to be closed by 2020, according to Christian Research, an organization that tracks religious trends in Britain. And there, where some of Jesus' original disciples preached the Gospel and planted the flag of the Kingdom of God, now few of the citizens consider themselves Born Again Christian believers. Why? The Victorian Society of the UK describes it like this: "Invariably, it seems churches become redundant. The country changes around them and for one reason or another they find themselves bereft of the worshipers needed to keep them going. Many, if not most, of the buildings seem eventually to find new uses...." [1]

One of the facts I found most interesting is the focus of the Committee on the Church Bells: "One of the Committee's guiding principles from the outset has been the need to save and not waste the value in almost every bell. This has been supported by both the policy of the Committee and the requirement of the Code of Practice associated with the Pastoral Measure. Both require that fittings from redundant churches should stay within their local area if at all possible. The recent advent of the Keltek Trust and the work of David Kelly have placed the day to day management and re-use of bell castings on a much broader and more comprehensive footing. A development endorsed by CfRB." [2]

Silent church bells! The solution offered by the Committee was to store them until a time in the future when someone might use them again. I suspect that, in Evangelical circles, many of our bells stopped ringing long ago, but no one noticed.

REDUNDANCY IN FRANCE AND IRELAND

According to Wikipedia, A 2004 IFOP (French Institute of Public Opinion) survey tallied that 44% of the French people do not believe in God; contrasted with 20% in 1947. [3]

Brian, a thirty-nine year old male in Dublin, Ireland, is studying psychotherapy and counseling at Dublin Business School. Brian reports, "I don't go to church, and I don't know one person who does. Fifteen years ago, I didn't know one person who didn't."

"CHRISTIANITY IN EUROPE COMING TO AN END"

This was the headline of an article written by Hilary White and posted by Lifesitenews.com on April 14, 2009. This article reported the warning by Cardinal Archbishop of Vienna that Christianity in Europe is dying out. Christoph Cardinal Schönborn said at St. Stephen's Cathedral on Easter Sunday, "The time of Christianity in Europe is coming to an end..." The article went on to report that the decline of the Catholic Church in Austria mirrors that of the rest of Europe since the advent of the 1960s "sexual revolution." While official Vatican statistics say that 72.7 percent of Austrians are Catholic, a 2005 European Social Survey found that just 63.9 percent of Austrians actually describe themselves as such and almost 30 percent say they have no religious affiliation at all. Weekly Mass attendance among Catholics in the country hovers around 10 percent and, between 1985 and 2002, the number of priests in Austria dropped by almost one-quarter.

Though many Europeans say they consider themselves Christians, far fewer actually attend services. One need only see the overwhelming number of gray-haired heads in church pews to know attendance will keep falling if something doesn't change dramatically. I cannot help but wonder why the Coalition for Redundant Churches (established specifically for the purpose of disposing of the property of redundant churches) did not, instead, try to discover and address the reason the churches were becoming redundant!

As I write this chapter I have just returned from Romania, where I have ministered on a somewhat regular basis since the mid-nineties. In 2000 my book, *"Stop GOING to Church"* was published in the Romanian language and has been distributed nationwide. Interestingly, when considering its publishing in their country, the editors there recommended removing the picture of the church building from the front cover in order to draw less fire from the religious leaders there who equate the building with the Church.

After working in Romania for many years, I still find that one of our greatest challenges is to persuade the Evangelical pastors there to place less emphasis on the building and more on the people. In certain areas of Romania it is not uncommon for evangelical pastors to be beaten, their buildings vandalized and equipment destroyed at the hands of thugs hired by local religious leaders. However, much of this tension could be avoided if the Evangelical leaders would simply avoid painting the word "Baserica" on the front of their buildings. In the minds of some of the non-Evangelical leaders and members, the Baserica is the only place to meet with God..and since, in the minds of most Romanians, the Orthodox Church is the only true church, any non-Orthodox structure is a false church and an affront to them.

Although, the idea of exchanging the word, "Baserica", for less offensive words, like "Fellowship" or "Christian Center" might seem foreign to some of our brethren there, those who are employing this strategy, combined with home-group discipleship, are discovering it is possible to build bridges rather than barriers with their Orthodox neighbors.

But, let me hasten to say that this plague is certainly not limited to Europe or the UK. My beloved homeland, the United States of America, has rapidly fallen victim to religious redundancy. A short time ago I had lunch with a State Overseer of a major denomination here in the South. He informed me that, out of more than four hundred churches he oversees, at least fifty have made the decision not to grow or move forward, and thus are dying. They obviously have given in to the spirit of redundancy. It is a growing problem here and around the world. Therefore, in this section we will take a close look at the situation at large, and consider ways to tear down the strongholds and free the captives.

David T. Olson, writing for the winter 2010 edition of Enrichment magazine reported, "While there are many signs of the church's evident success, in reality the American church is losing ground as the population continues to surge....The percentage of the population attending church on any given weekend has declined from 20.4 percent in 1990 to 17.0 percent in 2007" [4]

In his Enrichment article, I believe Mr. Olson's most compelling point was his assertion that "the decaying state of the American church tells us that the methods and pathways from 20 years ago are not as fruitful as they once were." So true! So why don't we change our methods? Because change can be frightening and even painful.

REDUNDANCY IN CHURCH MUSIC

To list the number and names of churches that have split over the music styles would require considerable space. But suffice it to say that too many sincere people have found themselves at odds with their fellow-parishioners over the music chosen for public worship. And, due to this challenge, church leaders around the world have chosen to become stagnant rather than rock the boat of the religious crowd. Those who insist on a weekend diet of eighteenth and nineteenth-century hymns seem to think that God exhausted his reservoir of creativity during that season of Church history.

Some time ago I spoke with a friend who had been invited to assist in the praise and worship of a traditional denominational Church in Oklahoma. The church has a strong history in the city and the pastor has ministered faithfully for the past twenty-five years. But, obviously something is awry. Over the past six months, no less than six staff members, including the Minister of Music, have resigned and moved on. The church has stopped growing and redundancy has become the norm, and no one is more aware of the need of change than the senior pastor. But, fear of rocking the boat has created paralysis. When the pastor spoke to my friend about assisting with the praise and worship, she suggested adjusting the number of singers on the team and expanding the styles of music they are currently using. This suggestion created immediate concern with the pastor, who feared making any changes that might upset the status quo and create unrest by his congregation and church board.

Sadly, this mentality continues to cripple and stagnate many churches all across our nation. Due to their need of positional security, many pastors balk at the idea of change, while their staff members and hungry parishioners move across town and join the new churches offering vibrant, life-giving contemporary expressions of praise and worship.

Unfortunately, I fear there is potential for a greater loss for church leaders who reject change. For according to the Bible, we shall all stand before God and give account of our actions here. How sad to think that we could run the risk of losing eternal rewards for the sake of preserving temporal comfort and provision.

I think I shall never forget sitting in a Sectional pastors' meeting within our denomination, back in the Eighties, listening to the morning speaker opine on the subject of adherence to the Word and rejecting compromise. He received spontaneous applause when he thundered against the neglect of hymnals and the use of choruses projected on the walls. In fact one of the more veteran pastors became so excited he stood to his feet and yelled "Amen, down with computers!"

TRAMPLING TRADITION

It is obvious that much of the controversy and the objection to change is due to the reluctance to challenge traditions we have held dear to our hearts. But, is it tradition we hold on to, or is it traditionalism? Perhaps, before we part company and split churches, we should distinguish between the two. On this subject, Jaroslav Pelikan wrote: "Tradition is the living faith of those now dead. Traditionalism is the dead faith of those now living."[5]

In an interview in U.S. News & World Report, Pelikan said: "Tradition is the living faith of the dead; traditionalism is the dead faith of the living. Tradition lives in conversation with the past, while remembering where we are and when we are and that it is we who have to decide. Traditionalism supposes that nothing should ever be done for the first time, so all that is needed to solve any problem is to arrive at the supposedly unanimous testimony of this homogenized tradition."[6]

At this season in my life, a considerable amount of my time is spent in consultation with church leaders. Some are seeking solutions to their debt load and insufficient income. Others want to know why their attendance is declining or why visitors do not stay. But, all too often I discover the fact that few leaders are willing to pay the price for change. It's one thing to diagnose our illness. It's another thing to receive a prescription to treat our illness. And, it's quite another thing to be willing to take the medicine required to cure our illness. If you're tired of standing still or walking the treadmill of redundancy, read on!

Chapter Two

The Bird Nest

One morning while eating breakfast, Georgiann and I watched a mother wren, just outside our kitchen window, lovingly feeding four of her children who had become so large their nest could barely hold them. Their bodies were no longer concealed as they had been for several weeks. It was evident to any observer that something had to change soon or there would be serious trouble for the baby birds, along with heartache and wasted energy for the mother.

Although we have repeatedly witnessed this cycle of love and life in this bird family, it took time for our eyes to be opened to the lesson God wanted to teach us. The scene we witnessed was sobering and enlightening. For many days and nights we observed this wren sitting on her nest in anticipation of another brood of babies. And we have witnessed, day after day, hour after hour Mrs. Wren bringing food to the new nest dwellers.

For several days we could not determine how many babies were there. But, as the babies grew, we could count four little beaks protruding upward from the nest...always open, ready to receive more food. However, on one particular morning the scene was different. The four babies were still there with their mouths opened wide. We could hear them crying out for more food. Their bodies had grown to the extent that there was no more room in the nest. When Mrs. Wren came to feed them, she could not sit on the edge and rest. She had to flutter her wings rapidly to hover long enough to deliver her food supply, then fly off again to gather more food for the hungry, impatient brood.

The situation at the Wren household was becoming critical. For not only was there no room for Mom Wren to stop, rest and communicate with her little ones, there was literally no more room for the babies. Their bodies were protruding over the edges of the nest, and they were literally sitting on top of each other. It was evident the time of their departure was at hand. Mom Wren knew there was a bigger world out there her little ones had not discovered.

Mom Wren knew the freedoms found outside the nest. She knew the joys of flying through the air, viewing God's creation and interacting with many others of the bird family; she also knew the joy of seeking out and discovering her own food, and the ultimate joy of building a new nest and bringing new little ones into God's world. However, she also knew the dangers ahead if her babies refused to leave the nest. Unless they left soon, there was real danger of one or more of them falling from the nest to the concrete below. Also, there was danger of one or more of them being crippled or suffocated by the weight of the others around them.

Without a doubt, it's a frightening thought to leave the nest. The babies are perched eight feet above a concrete floor. What if their wings don't really work? What if they fall? And if they do not fall, what will they face outside the nest? Would it not be better to just stay and be fed again and again in this place of security? There is really only one real choice. It is time to face the insecurity and the unknown. It is time to leave the nest and get out into the world. In reality, this is the Creator's plan. To ignore it and rebel against it will mean disease, discomfort and eventual death for the nest-dwellers.

Now, Georgiann and I know the lesson God wanted to teach us through the Wren family. After pastoring churches in the United States for more than thirty years, we have witnessed this scene repeatedly in the human family. Time and again we have seen the spiritual babies born in the church nests. We have witnessed faithful church leaders work tirelessly, Sunday after Sunday, month after month, year after year, bringing food to the hungry, growing and impatient children. Although many of the nest-dwellers have outgrown the nest and are getting on each other's nerves and invading their space, it is much easier to continue to sit there, with mouths open, demanding another meal, than to stretch their wings, leave the nest and fulfill their God-given destinies.

Oh, incidentally, I almost forgot to share the conversation I thought I overheard from the nest one day as I was leaving our home. Now, I make no boasts of being a linguist nor a dialectician. But, one cannot serve as a pastor for thirty years without distinctly recognizing the sounds of unrest and frustration in the nest. As I opened the front door of our home I stopped momentarily to try and determine why the baby birds were so upset. Then I thought I heard a frustrated conversation. One said, "It's so hot in here! Why doesn't someone air-condition this place?" Another chirped in, "This nest has become entirely too small for all of us. We need a new and larger nest." Another said, "I suggest we start a petition to build a new modern nest and while we're at it let's demand more feeding sessions during the week." Another even suggested finding someone else to feed them if their demands were not met. Then I heard what I believe was a word of wisdom. One of the nest-dwellers said, "Hey, this is ridiculous. God has blessed us so abundantly. He has given us parents who have lovingly given us shelter and daily provision. But, it's obvious we have now become a burden to them and to each other. Look, God has given each of us wings for a purpose. Let's spread our wings and fly!"

I had a schedule to keep and work to do, so I left. When I arrived home that day, the nest was empty. Another generation of young birds had left the security of their nest, spread their wings and began to soar into their God-given destinies. I couldn't help but wonder how much more rapidly we could expand the Kingdom of God if we would follow their examples.

All of us who claim an interest in outreach should remember that the word, OUTREACH, cannot be spelled without OUT. Out of the box, out of the nest, out of the shaker and out of the building!

We could learn much from the animal kingdom. For it seems the Creator put within them an innate ability to naturally do what is conducive to growth, maturity and reproduction. Unfortunately, many once vibrant churches have, either ceased to operate, or have settled into a state of redundancy rather than make the necessary changes to move forward. And further, all too often church leaders will allow the congregation to become career sermon-samplers rather than insisting they grow into mature disciples capable of reproducing. Career nest-dwellers would do well to study again the message Jesus delivered on "The light of the world." We will examine that message in our next chapter.

Chapter Three

The Light of the World

A fter delivering the message of the Beatitudes, Jesus instructed His disciples on their ministry on Earth. He described this ministry in very simplistic terms: "You are the salt of the earth and the light of the world."

The Beatitudes describe the character of the disciples. Salt and Light describe their influence. With that in mind, let's examine the purpose, the power and the place of Salt and Light Ministry.

According to the message of Jesus, the purpose of this ministry is to REpresent the Christ on Earth. When Jesus came to Earth, devotion to Jehovah God had been diluted by the religious leaders to little more than lifeless ritual. In other words, it had become redundant. Jesus brought life back into religion. He was the preservative that brought meaning back to the teachings of the Word of God, and He was the light that exposed the lies, the compromise and the hypocrisy of the religious leaders of His day.

His very life was light in a darkened world. When Jesus said "You Are the light", He was saying, "What I am, you will be. You will REpresent me. The things I do you will do also and greater..."

The salt of Christ in His people is the moral fiber...the only basis of purity and goodness on Earth. Take away the church and you take away the very presence that sustains and preserves goodness and points the way to God. But, how powerful are salt and light?

Natural salt has an amazing ability to preserve freshness and life and to prevent decay. Spiritual salt has the same ability in a human society. Natural light has the ability to dispel darkness and reveal objects that would, otherwise, be unnoticed by the natural eye. Likewise, spiritual light possesses the ability to dispel darkness and reveal the right path for us to take. Solomon said "There is a way that seems right to man but the end thereof are the ways of death." [7]

The author of Psalm 119:105 declared "Your Word is a lamp for my feet and a light for my path." Jesus said "I am the Way" (John 14:6). The Church is the light that points to the Way. John 3:19 records the words of Jesus, who declared, "Men love darkness because their deeds are evil." The light in the Church exposes the evil and reveals a solution in the Christ.

Light and darkness cannot coexist, for wherever light enters, darkness exits. But, what is this light Jesus spoke of? The light in us is the same that was resident in The Christ. His very presence changed the atmosphere around him. Likewise, the presence of the Church should change the atmosphere wherever it exists.

Remember, Jesus said, "I am the light of the world" (John 8:12). He later informed his disciples, "You are the light of the world" (Matthew 5:14). I admit I must have read those passages a thousand times before I received the revelation of the truth contained therein. Let's examine the word translated "*light*" in our Bibles.

Jesus declared Himself and His followers to be the light of the world. The word translated "*light*" in our English language is "*phos*" in the Greek language. By definition it is "a fire or light that cannot be kindled nor quenched." Contrasted with "*pheggos—a* reflection like the moon or planets", *phos* needs no kindling nor reflection, for it is literally the light of God. Phos comes from the very presence and nature of God. I'm not even sure we can grasp the power of this truth without revelation from the Holy Spirit, but let me try to illustrate it.

In the beginning, when creating the universe, God said "Let there be light", and there was. But, what was the source of the light? The source was God, Himself. He did not need an external source for the light was in Him. I believe this is precisely the reason there will be no need for artificial light in heaven. For the Lamb of God will be the light. John wrote of his vision in the Revelation, "...the city had no need of the sun, neither of the moon, to shine in it: for the glory of God did lighten it, and the Lamb is the light thereof." (Rev. 21:23)

Scientists tell us that the universe is ever-expanding. Perhaps this is due to the fact that the words of God are everlasting. Therefore, when God commanded "Let there be light", the creative power of His words, just continue producing light.

Although God's light cannot be kindled nor quenched, it apparently can be hidden. Jesus warned against hiding the light under a basket. It is for this reason that I believe many churches could cease to exist and their surrounding communities would not miss them, for their light has been contained under the basket of the church. This is totally contrary to the ministry and the mission of Jesus, who said, "Let your light so shine before men that they may see your good works and praise your Father in heaven." These words of Jesus illustrate clearly where the light is to shine. Our works are not IN HERE but OUT THERE. However, if we are not careful we will spend so much time in the shaker and under the bowl that we have no time nor opportunity to be effective in the place we are called to be.

The command was "Go into the world and present the Good News" or "Go into the darkness and present the light." Too often we become salt and then want to stay in the shaker. The purpose of Salt is not to preserve the church but to preserve and promote the Kingdom of God in the midst of the kingdom of darkness. The salt is not effective until it is comes out of the shaker. Likewise, the light has no effect on the darkness until it is removed from its covering.

When I am speaking publicly on this subject, I love to ask the audience where light is least effective. Light is obviously most effective in the presence of darkness, not in the presence of light. To illustrate this, turn on a flashlight in a well-lighted room and note how little effect it has. But, turn on the same flashlight in a darkened room and witness the powerful effect of light.

The intended message is this: The birds who insist on staying in the nest will never reach their potential or affect their world. Likewise, professing Christians and church members whose lives consist of church meetings, sermons and "bless me" sessions, will never positively impact the darkness of the world around them.

Jesus was criticized for daring to move outside the comfort zone of the religious saltshaker and the temple basket. And his response to His accusers was "Those who are sick need a physician." If we could simulcast a message from Jesus Christ to His Church next Sunday, I wonder what His message would be. Very possibly it would include, "You are the salt, get out of the shaker. You are the light of the world not the light of the church. Take the light out there and penetrate the darkness!"

Most likely, every Evangelical church that has ever existed was launched with a passion to reach the unconverted and to make disciples of Jesus Christ. However, it is just as likely that every congregation has faced the crossroads of Comfort and Conviction or Progress and Paralysis. At some point in the life of every local church, a decision is made to become introverted and maintain status quo or pay the price for a renewed passion and cultural connection. When the leaders of any church opt for comfort and status quo, the common strategy is to circle the wagons and attempt to develop a "Christian" community isolated and insulated from the contamination of the heathen outside. This results in what Dan Buck referred to as the "faith Ghetto." In the premiere issue of Relevant Magazine, Dan presented an article titled, "Getting out of the Faith Ghetto."[8]

In this article, Dan Buck says what is occurring in the church is "the creation of a ghetto." According to this article, the word "ghetto" has long since been associated with an inner city housing project, but ghettoes have been around since the middle ages. Back then there were walled sections of a city that a religious group, usually Jews, was forced to occupy as a way of keeping them from the rest of the population. Christians appear to be doing it to themselves.

Why would he say that? And if it is true, why would the church do that? It seems counter-productive to the purpose of the church. Let's look at what Mr. Buck had to say in defense of his statement.

"Opening a phone book, I can find Christian pharmacies, Christian art framing and Christian bakeries, and here in my hometown, someone has created a business concept of a cheesy Christian t-shirt. The Lord's Gym Health and Fitness centers are dedicated to promoting "Fitness for Body and Soul" and offer classes such as Praise Dance, Body of Armor and Chariots of Fire Spin. Now, some might argue such businesses are a good model of stretching the barriers of our spiritual activity beyond Sunday morning. However, all they are doing is adding spiritual language into things that are naturally spiritual. Because they are part of the human experience God has created. Taking care of your body is spiritual even if you don't play the newsboys while working on your biceps. These *Christian* shops are doing what all the *secular* shops are doing, but to the exclusion of non-believers. Creating places like this completely removes God's disciples from the world, which doesn't bode well for the world and I daresay, ends up hurting the church as well."[9]

My personal struggle with the concept of the *Christian Ghetto* began back in the late seventies. Georgiann and I were serving in our first pastorate in a Los Angeles suburb, called Lakewood. Although I was in my early thirties, God had graced me with enough talent and anointing as a communicator and musician to attract people who wanted more than liturgical ritual. Further, my regular appearance as a music vocalist on the Trinity Broadcasting Network drew numerous guests to our meetings. Therefore, our church became a magnet for church members looking for lively praise and worship and strong, "no-compromise" preaching. Consequently, in a few short years, our congregation more than tripled and morphed into a vibrant group of happy saints. Then it happened! I had an encounter with God that shook me to the very core of my soul and spirit.

One morning, I arrived at the office early and entered the auditorium to spend some quiet time before engaging the activities of the day. As usual, I began walking around the auditorium and praying. I walked around every row of pews, laying my hands on each row as I prayed. But that morning something was different. As I walked and prayed, I could visualize the faces of most of the people who sat there each Sunday. And though I was thankful for the faithful attendees, I felt a deep sadness I could not explain. Then, out of the deepest recesses of my soul, I began to cry out, "God, I am not satisfied to just preach and sing to saved and sanctified people week after week. I want to see the broken, the sick, the lonely and desperate, sitting in these pews! How can we reach them?" Then, I felt the strongest impression to walk to an exit facing the street and to open the door.

As I responded to the impression, I opened the door and found myself looking straight at our church sign facing Candlewood Street. Then God began to challenge me with a series of questions that would dramatically alter my life and the direction of our church. I cannot say I heard an audible voice, but I do know that I experienced the following dialogue with God. He challenged me with a series of questions and observations that went something like this:

God: "What is the message printed on the sign?"

Me: "First Assembly of God Church".

God: "Isn't it a bit arrogant to declare your church the *first, the premiere, number one* church in Lakewood?" (Then as if to challenge my education as an English major in college, I was reminded that the definition of *church* and *assembly* are basically synonymous, so the message of the sign was not only arrogant, but redundant!)

Me: "God, what are you trying to say to me?"

God: "This area is filled with people who are spiritually dying, and you will never reach them by promoting yourself as the "Premiere" gathering of Christians in Lakewood. I want this church to become a Life Center."

I was so shaken by the encounter with God that I went back inside the auditorium and began to weep as I envisioned the sad, lonely and broken souls I had driven by week after week on the streets of Greater Long Beach. I was so moved by the experience that I went to my office and asked my secretary to call a meeting with our church board the following Sunday night after our church meeting.

Following the Sunday night meeting, I met with our church board in my office and shared with them the message I felt God had challenged me with. Then, I recommended that we begin the process of changing the name of our church to *The Life Center*. To my amazement, the board members agreed that God had indeed spoken to me. A few weeks later, I shared the same message with the entire congregation. The Spirit of God moved powerfully in the meeting as our hearts were broken for the lost, the hurting and the dying around us. A short time later, not only was the sign changed, but our lives were changed to become individual life centers, and life-givers to those around us.

I will not tell you the process was instant or easy. To become a Life Center meant we had to lose people to gain others. Unwittingly, in our zeal and excitement, we had become a Christian Ghetto, happy to meet at least three times per week and conduct meetings for Christians, while neglecting the true mission of the Church.

Perhaps you question whether God really challenged me about our church sign, and if He really even cares about such earthly matters. If so, let me challenge you with this: If the mission of the Church is to introduce unbelievers to Christ and make disciples of them, which church sign best communicates to those we are called to reach? *"First Church of the Reborn, Holy Ghost, Fire Baptized Believers"* or *"The Hope Center?"* Just sayin!

Let me be crystal clear at this point. No one should assume your church will automatically transition from introversion to outreach by changing the name of your church. Like water baptism, this is an outward sign of a necessary inner transformation. Yes, signs MAY need to be changed. But, more importantly, hearts MUST be changed, and attitudes and opinions must be altered to conform to the heart of God for those still outside the family.

What God burned into my spirit back in the Seventies, burns even brighter today. In what many now call the *"Post-Christian"* era, it is imperative that we dismantle the Christian Ghettos and open our doors and hearts to those Christ called and commissioned us to reach.

I will readily admit that after four decades of ministry, I have little patience with Pharisees in the church, and therefore, make no apologies for offending them. I think I've grown too old to concern myself with my critics, and I am quite sure I'm not on the radar of a "pulpit committee" interested in enticing a successful shepherd to greener pastures. Therefore, I will say it like it is! Christian ghettos stink! And the longer a congregation exists, the more likely it is to become ghettoized! Further, the longer a church is allowed to remain introverted and redundant, the more wicked and un-like Christ it will be become.

In his book *Deep and Wide,* Andy Stanley is painfully transparent when he relates the childhood experience of watching a deacon punch his father in the face at a church business meeting. I have no doubt that story brought back very painful memories for PK's (pastor's kids) with similar experiences of witnessing their parents slapped, kicked and/or called "SOBs" by church members. Fortunately for himself and for the Church at large today, by the grace of God, Andy Stanley was strengthened to overcome that painful experience. But sadly, hundreds of the young converts have become casualties of the Ghetto and the Pharisees living there.

For those of you who find yourself residing in the *faith ghetto,* I urge you to escape while there is time. And for those of you who may have been taken captive by the Pharisee spirit, I urge you to admit it, repent, break out of the ghetto, lay down your agenda, and join His!

If you think I'm too hard on the modern-day Pharisees, I remind you of the saying "It takes one to know one", and I readily confess I am a recovering Pharisee. And were it not for God's grace and my support group, I would still fall off the wagon! In my humble opinion, every transitioning church needs a small group for Recovering Pharisees.

TAKING THE LIGHT OUTSIDE

In 2002 I resigned as pastor of Life Center in Russellville, Arkansas. Since the church was formed in 1990, we had become a shaker full of happy salt and baskets full of great light, in a city with more than thirty salt shakers and light baskets within a five-mile radius, and where more than fifty percent of the citizens had no church affiliation. Prior to my resignation, our media teams conducted "on the street" interviews, posing this question: "What do you think of when we say 'church'?" The young said "boring"; the middle aged said "not relevant"; and the older said "hypocrites". Based on our research, our church leaders made a critical decision to alter our methodology in presenting the Gospel.

When our son, Steve, assumed my position as senior pastor in January of 2002, we had 289 grains of salt in our congregation. By January of 2007, we had 399. By January of 2008, the number had grown to 539. One year later it was 676, and at the time of this writing, the congregation has grown to over 1300 on two campuses. One of the newcomers to our church family is a physician who watched the meetings online for six weeks. When asked what brought him to us, he responded "I found life here." All around us there are thousands of people searching for life. They will not find it in ritual and redundancy, but in the presence of light-bearers.

Chapter Four

Jesus Got Out of the Van

I n August of 2009, I took a team to Romania to participate in a pastors' conference in the region of Oltenia. On Sunday morning, I was riding with the host pastor and his wife to a neighboring village where I was to speak to one of nine congregations under his purview. On our journey to the church meeting, we drove through a village where the streets were crowded with masses of people of all ages. When I asked where these crowds were going, my host said, "They're going to the market." He then informed me that the market was held in that village every Sunday.

We drove just a few more miles and arrived at our destination, a small white building with the words "Baserica Pentecostal" painted across the front. The small building was already filled with forty faithful church members ready to worship and hear the guest speaker from America. The praise and worship was lively and inspiring, led by a young lady with a guitar. During the time of announcements, I panned the congregation and counted thirty-two ladies and eight men in attendance. I was aware that several of the men were living outside Romania, trying to earn a living for their families. But, the remainder of those missing were among the thousands of unconverted men who consider church to be for women and children.

I was well received by the congregation that morning, and I was impressed by their sincere worship. But during the course of the meeting, I experienced a strange impression. My mind flashed back to our journey through the crowded market to arrive at the little white building. As I pondered this, I imagined the pastor, his wife, Jesus and I riding in the van, enjoying fellowship along the way. But in my imagination, I heard Jesus suddenly say, "Stop the van! Stop the van!" And as the driver pulled to the side of the street and stopped, Jesus got out of the van and immediately began to mingle among the people.

As we left the little white church building and began to drive home, I said, "Milo, let me tell you what happened this morning. We went to church, but Jesus got out of the van at the market." Milo, said "What do you mean?" I explained that I felt if Jesus had been riding with us that morning, he could not have resisted getting out of the van and ministering to the people at the market, because that was His stated purpose. Jesus said "Those who are healthy do not need a physician. I did not come to minister to the righteous, but to the unrighteous."[10] I then shared my opinion that we had traveled through the crowded marketplace, filled with masses of broken and sick people, to get to the little church building where I ministered to forty healthy believers.

Milo was both surprised and intrigued by my comment. Then I challenged him further when I suggested the possibility of stretching a tent in the marketplace on Sunday mornings, and offering cold water and encouragement for the shoppers along with food, activities, and Bible stories for the children while their parents shopped. I am happy to report that Milo was excited about the outreach possibilities I mentioned and, at this writing, the marketplace ministry has been established.

In 2010, a year after I challenged Milo with the idea of Marketplace Ministry, I returned to the Oltenia area with Missionary-Evangelist Ed Huie and Cary McVay, the children's pastor for our local church. After a long flight, we arrived at Pastor Milo's house late on Saturday evening. As we were preparing to retire for the evening, Milo informed us we had to rise early the next morning. When we inquired why, he informed us we had to be at the market by 8 AM. I could hardly contain my excitement when we drove into the crowded market and found that Milo's teams had preceded us, erected tents and set up tables filled with food, coffee,

31

tea, and literature. Cary McVay taught the team members to create balloon animals and to paint the faces of the children. By noon that Sunday morning, the teams had handed out candy, cookies, bread, water, coffee, and tea to thousands of shoppers, and had personally distributed more than fifteen hundred New Testaments. As we were preparing to leave the market, an elderly member of Milo's congregation approached me and said, "Pastor Larry, I want you to know that I read your book, *Stop Going to church*, but this is the first time I have ever witnessed it in action."

I am happy to report that Milo and his congregation are continuing to carry on the marketplace ministry and are now expanding into other villages as they take the light into the darkness around them. As I reflect on what Milo is doing in Oltenia, Romania, I am reminded of a situation Georgiann and I encountered in Florida several years ago.

Georgiann and I were invited to Florida to meet with a small home group considering launching a church. After our meeting with the group, one of the couples provided Georgiann and me with a tour of the surrounding area and its multi-million dollar mansions. As we drove through one of the beautifully landscaped neighborhoods, one of our hosts asked, "How can we get these people to our church?" My immediate response was, "I think you're asking the wrong question. I believe a better question is how can we get the church to these people?"

While Pastor Milo and I discussed the radical outreach ideas in Romania, I couldn't help but reflect on our own church programs here at home. I have no doubt that multitudes of broken sick people are bypassed and ignored each week as we healthy believers rush to our designated meeting places. I illustrated this scenario in chapter three of *Stop Going to Church*. In that chapter, I paraphrased Acts 3:1-9 as follows:

One day, Peter and John were going to church at the time of prayer at three o'clock in the afternoon. Now a man crippled from birth was being carried to the temple gate called Beautiful where he was put everyday to beg from those going to church. When he saw Peter and John about to enter, he asked them for money. Peter looked straight at him, as did John. Then Peter said, "Look at us." So the man gave them his attention, expecting to get something from them. Then Peter said, "Silver and gold I do not have, but such as I have, I give to you."

"Here's a flyer announcing our annual revival meeting down at the church. We have the world-renowned evangelist I.B. Awesome with us and man can he preach! Listen, service times are at 10 AM and 6 PM. You just wait right here and our bus will pick you up and bring you to church." Taking him by the right hand, Peter shook his hand and said, "Now don't miss the big pink bus." Peter and John continued merrily on their way with a sense of encouragement that they had an opportunity to share the gospel by inviting a needy man to church.

At 9:30 AM as the big pink bus lumbered toward the gate called Beautiful, the beggar shuffled along the sidewalk to the curb and began to wave furiously for the bus to stop. Unfortunately, the bus driver, distracted by two of his juvenile passengers throwing spit wads, turned the steering wheel too sharply, struck the curb, taking the life of the beggar before he had an opportunity to go to church.

Fortunately for the crippled man, the story did not end the way I paraphrased it. Peter and John took the Church to the man in need as Christ intended. How many of us have been guilty of "going to church" instead of "being the Church?" How many of us are guilty of hearing the Word rather than doing the Word? We must remember that nowhere in the Word is anyone commanded to go to church. But Jesus emphatically commanded the Church to go to the world. However, it is easier to agree with this premise than to implement it. For to implement it often requires radical alterations in our traditional programs and schedules, and will possibly require us to sacrifice several of our religious cows.

Probably nowhere is "Going to church" more obvious than here in the center of the *Bible Belt.* As a chaplain for the Pope County Sheriff's Office, I often ride with deputies on Sunday evenings. As we cruise the county, we pass small church buildings with less than a dozen cars in the parking lot, and we pass large church buildings surrounded by hundreds of vehicles that transported the saints to hear yet another sermon. And while these faithful church members are gathered for another "service", we are being dispatched to scenes of domestic violence, robberies, child abuse, and suicides. I cannot help but wonder how these scenes would change if our churches would conduct fewer meetings for the saints inside and more services for the seekers outside!

Chapter Five

I Shall Not Be Moved

Redundancy and reluctance to change are not limited to any generation. Three thousand years ago, God addressed the problem through the prophet, Amos. Listen to his rebuke: "I can't stand your religious meetings. I'm fed up with your conferences and conventions. I want nothing to do with your religion projects, your pretentious slogans and goals. I'm sick of your fund-raising schemes, your public relations and image making. I've had all I can take of your noisy ego-music. When was the last time you sang to me? Do you know what I want? I want justice—oceans of it. I want fairness—rivers of it. That's what I want. That's all I want." [11]

If either Amos or Isaiah could come back and visit our world today, they probably would be in great demand as guest speakers in our churches. Just the thought of having a renowned prophet such as Amos would pack the pews of most of our churches. However, if he were given the opportunity to speak in many of our 4S churches (Saved, Sanctified, Satisfied, and Sleepy), I suspect Amos would be a one-time guest speaker, for the brother had a habit of "telling it like it is!" And in far too many locations, "like it is" is "like it was" when God thundered against the religious redundancy of the past.

God's stern warning through Isaiah is recorded in The Message as follows: "Quit your worship charades. I can't stand your trivial religious games, monthly conferences, weekly sabbaths, special meetings; meetings, meetings, meetings. I can't stand one more. Meetings for this, meetings for that...I hate them. You have worn me out...I'm sick of your religion, religion, religion, while you go right on sinning. When you put on your next prayer performance, I'll be looking the other way...no matter how long or loud or often you pray...I'll not be listening and do you know why? Because you have been tearing people to pieces and your hands are bloody. Go home and wash up, clean up your act, sweep your lives clean of your evildoings so I don't have to look at them any longer. Say no to wrong. Learn to do good. Work for justice. Help the down and out. Stand up for the homeless and go to bat for the defenseless." [12]

And finally, note the words of Jesus recorded by Matthew: "And when you pray, do not keep on babbling like pagans, for they think they will be heard because of their many words." [13]

When Jesus entered the human realm, religious ritual and formalism was so entrenched in society that His message and methodology sparked a murderous riot among the religious leaders. The same has been true down through the centuries. Countless churches have suffered discord and destruction, and countless spiritual leaders have been denigrated and discouraged when changes were suggested that threatened the status quo of the organization or its members.

During the late sixties, I was traveling with a college buddy named Alton Garrison. Working as an evangelistic team, Alton served as the primary speaker and I served as the musical vocalist. During one of our ministry tours, we spent several days in revival meetings in a small church in Laramie, Wyoming.

To say the congregation there was set in their ways would be a tremendous understatement. As the vocalist, it was my assignment to try and create a worshipful, receptive atmosphere in which the congregation could receive the message Alton had prepared for them. But I found my assignment in Laramie to be especially challenging due to one particular woman. This female pillow (spelling deliberate) of the church always sat conspicuously on the front row where she could visibly display her disapproval of anything that did not fit her preferences. Whether I sang up-tempo or slow songs, she scowled, with her fingers in her ears. I thought possibly my amplifier was too loud so I continued lowering the volume until eventually I was singing with no amplification. But it made no difference to Sister Cynic. Her attitude seemed to be "Son, I've seen and heard it all, and nothing you can say or do is going to move me!" I was so personally moved by her attitude and her actions that, between services, I rewrote the lyrics to an old hymn many of you will recognize.

Sung to the tune of I Shall Not Be Moved:

I'm satisfied right where I am, I shall not be moved
Though the Spirit moves again, I shall not be moved
I'll sit right here and hinder those around me, and I shall not be moved

The Preacher wore that striped shirt he knows I do not like
I wish that I had stayed at home, Gunsmoke's on tonight
But, I'll sit right here and grieve the Holy Spirit and
I shall not be moved.

I'll stand right up and testify of what God's done for me
But when they pass the offering plate I'll act like I don't see
I can't afford to give God what He asks for, So I shall not be moved

I've heard that same old message a hundred times or more
He says the Lord is coming. .He's even at the door
I wonder now if my heart is ready, but I shall not be moved

He says there'll be a rapture, the saints of God shall rise
Caught up to meet the Savior and dwell with Him on high
Now I'm afraid I'm not really ready, But I shall not be moved

CHORUS
I shall not be, I shall not be moved
I shall not be, I shall not be moved
If Christ should come before I leave this service…
I shall not be moved!

(The Singing Deweys recorded the song and added the following chorus)

Please Lord Jesus Help me to be moved
Please Lord Jesus Help me to be moved
For when you come I want to be ready to make that final move!

That masterpiece was eventually published and recorded by several Southern Gospel groups and became a major hit, selling at least a hundred copies nationwide! (Thanks Mom!) Sadly, the truth of those lyrics is too close for comfort in many churches, where we tend to place higher value on our preferences, opinions, and traditions than on God's plan for His Church and His Kingdom. And when we succumb to our personal desires, it's easy to slip into rebellion and contribute to the cycle of redundancy.

CHAPTER SIX

The Pain of Change

B ack in the Seventies, when God began to stir my heart concerning the true identity and mission of His Church, I had no idea where that revelation would lead me. It began in a small Assemblies of God fellowship in Lakewood, California. It was our first pastorate and the congregation there was unbelievably gracious to me and Georgiann.

During those formative years, they were patient and longsuffering with us as young parents and embryonic church leaders. But even then, the pain of change was evident. From changing the name of our church to the use of overhead projectors and Scripture songs during praise and worship, few, if any of us, could escape the suspicions of compromise and/or loss of our traditions.

Young men like Larry Gregory received the revelation and could no longer be content to attend church meetings, sing songs, and hear sermons. The fire began to burn in Larry's heart to the extent he left our fellowship and moved to San Pedro where he launched a ministry to the unconverted. Then our youth pastors, Steve and Gaye Vanzant, responded to the call and "deserted" us to launch an outreach in an abandoned theater in East Los Angeles.

The fact that other young couples felt the need to follow these new missionaries temporarily evoked feelings of abandonment by me and Georgiann, and stirred rumors of schism among some of the congregants. But today, we look back on those years with gratitude. Larry and Linda Gregory went on to serve as missionaries in the South Pacific and now lead a thriving soul-winning congregation in Florida. And for the past eighteen years, Steve and Gaye Vanzant have led a strong outreach church in Fort Worth, Texas, where Steve has become the chaplain for the Haltom City Fire Department, and has authored an inspiring book, titled, *The Significance of One*. No doubt, these stories would be quite different had we not all endured the pain of change.

The pain of change we experienced at First Assembly of God in Lakewood, California resulted in a transition into an extroverted congregation that grew numerically from 100 to over 800, with four weekend meetings in a new facility constructed debt-free in a season when mortgage interest reached 22.5%. I would have been happy to spend the rest of my life and ministry with that wonderful congregation. However, God had other plans and was not finished stretching me and Georgiann.

In January of 1987, Georgiann and I responded to the call from a historical church in Arkansas. Located in the heart of the Bible Belt, this church had enjoyed over seventy years of strong witness in the region. But the church had undergone a severe trial and leadership failure, and the church board asked if we would consider coming for a weekend of ministry and interviews. I assured them that we were content in California, but out of love and compassion for our many friends in the congregation, we would provide a weekend of ministry and trust God to bring the encouragement they needed.

During the weekend that Georgiann and I returned to visit and serve as pulpit guests, I did everything I could to bring encouragement to the congregation, and everything I could to persuade the church board and congregation that we were not relocating to become their pastors. In fact, in the Sunday morning meeting, I chided them for the apparent lack of numerical growth over the thirteen years since we had resigned as their ministers of youth and music. I tried to assure them, that if I were to become their pastor, I would never allow them to become content with the status quo of conducting church meetings for "satisfied saints", but would constantly challenge them to reach the lost. To my amazement, the challenge I delivered was well-received and the Holy Spirit moved in a powerful manner as many people responded in re-dedication and re-commitment of their lives to the expansion of the Kingdom.

Reluctantly, we agreed to a vote of confidence and, following another powerful meeting on Sunday night, the congregation responded with a vote of 96%. The board had advised me earlier that, due to the shattered, confused state of the congregation, we should not expect a strong vote of confidence. Therefore, when the votes were tallied, we were all shocked and were convinced that surely God was involved in the transition of their lives and ours.

As much as we loved our church family in California, Georgiann and I knew in our hearts we had to respond to the call to Arkansas. So, in January of 1987, we turned over the reins of the church in Lakewood to Chuck and Ruth Atherton, who had served on staff with us for several years.

The first twelve months of the ministry honeymoon in Arkansas were rewarding as the congregation began to respond to my messages of forgiveness, healing, and encouragement. We implemented a successful discipleship course, out of which over three hundred graduated. Additionally, our praise and worship began to become more Scripture-centered and less Hymnal-bound. We reconfigured our Sunday school curricula to include subjects to address contemporary issues such as divorce, blended families, etc. We even went so far as to change the decor and alter the seating arrangement in some of our classrooms. And, in an effort to reach out to the hundreds of teenagers cruising our streets on weekends, we scheduled Friday night concerts, offering music they could identify with. Consequently, we began to experience the pain of change.

The nationally-acclaimed discipleship course was labeled "brain-washing" by a few opponents; the more contemporary praise and worship was criticized as "non-spiritual"; The Sunday school curricula was labeled "worldly," and I was informed by one of the senior saints that a newbie had taken his favorite seat so he would no longer attend; And finally, our Friday night youth concerts were categorized as compromise and a lowering of our traditional standards.

The fact that our youth group was growing, and increasing numbers of teenagers were responding to the concerts and to the love of God, seemed insignificant in light of our soiled carpets, broken chairs, and our necessary associations with the unchurched. Then, a gentleman in the church presented me with an ultimatum, threatening to completely destroy me unless I resigned the pastorate. His precise words were, "Larry Pyle, you are no match for me. I've taken down bigger men than you, and I will destroy you unless you resign and leave here." His words shocked me, for we had been friends for more than sixteen years. His children had grown up under our youth and music ministries. We had traveled together and had worked side by side to advance our ministry to the children in our community. Further, while I served in youth and music ministry, this man had supplied the gasoline for my automobile and had befriended my family on many occasions. Now, I sat stunned as my former sidekick, friend, and supporter threatened to destroy me. But, what was more sobering than the identity of the speaker were the words he spoke.

SAME SPIRIT—DIFFERENT MESSENGER

Before moving from California, our outreach ministries had penetrated the street culture to the extent that some in the "Gay" Community and the Occult circles had felt threatened, and I began to receive phone calls threatening my life, the life of my children, and the safety of our church. Many of the phone threats were recorded and were sobering in nature, but one message stood out above all the rest. The demoniac making the phone threats said, "Larry Pyle, you are no match for me. I will destroy you!" Now, years later and fifteen hundred miles from California, I sat listening to one I had considered my friend and coworker, using the identical words to threaten me. I knew immediately that the man sitting in front of me issuing the threats was not my enemy. My enemy was none other than the one the Apostle Paul described when he penned this message to believers in Ephesus: "We do not wrestle against flesh and blood, but against principalities, against powers, against the rulers of the darkness of this world, against spiritual wickedness in high places" (Ephesians 6:12).

On numerous occasions, I met with and tried to make peace with the man who threatened to destroy me, but to no avail. And true to his threats, over the next twenty four months, I found myself hauled into ecclesiastical court at least quarterly to defend my integrity and my ministry. Finally, when it seemed I could no longer effectively lead the congregation I had felt called to, I met with fellow-pastors and spiritual elders of our city. I explained to them my dilemma and requested their prayer and counsel. I poured out my heart, sharing with them my desire to lead our church family in evangelism and discipleship. But if I stayed, there would be further accusations, hearings, and further confusion to the new converts we were reaching on a regular basis. However, if we moved away, I would leave knowing God had called us to the heart of the Bible Belt to blow a trumpet in Zion, to awake those who slept, and to reach those who were yet unreached. The elders of our city prayed with me and unanimously counseled me to stay in the city and start over. I even traveled to New York to visit with a spiritual mentor I trusted implicitly. After listening to me at length, my counselor in New York said, "Brother, if you forsake them, the sheep will scatter... leave the building and pastor the Church."

The decision to resign was heart-rending for me and my family. Prior to my resignation, I counseled my staff not to follow me, but to follow God and seek Him for their own destinies. Then, on the Sunday I announced my resignation, I informed the congregation of my decision to remain in the city and requested that each of them pray and find God's will for their own lives. Although it was an extremely difficult decision, and one I would not want to repeat, I had followed what I felt was God's will for my life. And I had followed the counsel of the elders of our city. However, my decision to remain in the city and to launch a new church caused me to break fellowship with the denomination Georgiann and I both loved, and had grown up in. It was a difficult and painful season for me, for my family, and for the denominational leaders I had worked with. (I am pleased to report at this writing that our fellowship has been restored and we are again working as a team).

CHAPTER SEVEN

Starting Over

In June of 1990, Life Center was launched in the Gardner Junior High School Auditorium with the stated mission of reaching the unconverted, disconcerted, hurting, and confused souls in our area. After months of meetings in the high school auditorium, we moved into an abandoned bowling alley, filled with unspeakable debris. Utilizing a front-end loader, we pushed the debris out the back door of the building. Then we purchased theater seats from an abandoned theater in Paris, Arkansas. We ordered new fabric and the ladies of our church reupholstered the seats.

We initially rented the ugly building for $250 per month and over the next twelve months, we established effective youth and children's ministries. Our praise and worship team was powerful and began to travel around the nation in ministry; our attendance grew to the point that we needed an additional morning meeting; and with great unity and dedication we poured countless hours, energy, and $50,000 into the renovation of the facility. A new and effective outreach had been born and a community eyesore had been redeemed and restored. In fact, on the first anniversary of our lease, the owner of the building was so impressed with the work we had done that he raised our rent from $250 to $2500 per month. At that point, our church leadership team began searching for a place we could call our own.

The next few years were both challenging and rewarding for the new outreach called the Life Center. We purchased eight acres of undeveloped property along Interstate 40, and in early 1993, we broke ground for our new facility. Our congregation continued to grow and in early 1994, we moved into our new 20,000 square foot building. In the months to come, our new neighbors would become Sonic, Lowes, a Day Care Center, a Veterinary Clinic, a new Post Office, and several other Governmental facilities. And again, our congregation began to grow to the point that we needed additional meeting times to accommodate the crowds who came to hear speakers such as Tommy Tenney, Clint Brown, and other well-known revivalists.

As the news of our work and our celebrity speakers spread, hungry Christians drove for many miles and lined up outside our doors for hours, anxious to receive another spiritual touch. It was not uncommon for our meetings to last four to five hours, with people wanting to just stay and bask in the presence of God. It was a glorious season, and I admit, I enjoyed it as much as anyone. But I was troubled by the fact that we could, and would, drive for hours to experience more of God's manifest presence, but had little or no thought of reaching the unconverted around us. I had a sense that many of us were missing God's purpose behind the season of joy and refreshing, and I began again to share with our congregation the conviction that we had to avoid introversion and take Him to the streets.

During our first ten years, we had constructed and moved into our own new building adjacent to I-40, and we had experienced great seasons of revival spirit and unity. However, by the year 2000, my spirit had become troubled over what I called the *Status Quo* syndrome. Now, I know it is better defined as the *Redundancy Syndrome*. Within ten years, we had evolved into a saved, sanctified and satisfied church, happy and anxious to gather each week to enjoy great praise and worship and an encouraging message to get us through another week. I felt we had become precisely what God had instructed me not to build...another *ordinary*, introverted church. Sadly, we had become trapped again in the cycle of redundancy. So with that nagging at my spirit, I began to take action.

Early in 2000, I met with our pastoral staff members and shared my feelings. I loved our congregation. I was happy with what God had done over the first ten years. But I was unhappy that we were quickly becoming introverted. I told the staff members that I just could not continue conducting meetings for Christians. Our baptistery had been dry too long, and we had to do something to reach the unconverted. As I shared my burden with the staff members, our youth pastor (our son, Steve) and our Missions Director, Jerry Shaffer, suggested we try something different. In fact, they asked permission to launch a Saturday night meeting, aimed specifically at young families.

I knew from demographic statistics, that 65 percent of the families surrounding us were under the age of thirty-five, and were significantly untouched by the large number of churches in our area. So, when the younger staffers suggested we start something new and different, I sensed God was shaking our nest again, and I consented.

A few days later, our staff met with our elders and we shared the concept of the Saturday night meeting to be called "Saturday Night Life". Everyone seemed to share the excitement of something new and different. However, few of us understood just how the excitement and the "difference" would affect us in the days to come.

In January of 2001, Saturday Night Life was launched with great anticipation and much prayer. The younger staffers had asked me to give them enough rope to hang themselves and, after the first meeting, I understood why. In the weeks prior to the SNL launch, the guys had gone into the local coffeehouses and youth/music venues and had recruited a new band, made up of very talented, sandal-clad individuals with interesting hairdos and questionable spiritual commitment.

To say the first SNL meeting was different would be an understatement. The auditorium lights were dimmed. The music was uncomfortably loud. Snacks were served before and after the meeting and were actually brought into the auditorium. (*"Sanctuary"* for those of you who have not read *Stop Going to Church*) Without a doubt, thoughts of "Sanctuary Desecration" flashed through the minds of several of us more mature saints. Nevertheless, contrary to some of our opinions and preferences, something fresh was being born right before our eyes, and God was about to expand our spiritual vision and worldview in a manner we had not expected.

Over the next few months, we began to witness some strange, but encouraging events. Some of the young and "questionable" band members who had been recruited from the local youth hangouts were experiencing the anointed presence of God for the first time. As music lovers, they had simply accepted an invitation to play another gig, but they loved the atmosphere and the "feeling", and asked permission to play on a regular schedule. And, as they continued to come and participate in SNL, one by one, the unconverted band members began to surrender their lives to Christ.

To those of us who grew up under the influence of the Happy Goodmans, the Blackwood Brothers, and the Gaithers, the music was strange and uncomfortably loud. But we couldn't deny that God was present and changing lives. One thirty-something, who had been out of church for almost twenty years, came and sat in his truck for two weeks, listening to the sounds of contemporary praise and worship pouring through the walls of our building. On the third week, he sat at a table in the rear of the auditorium, drinking a cup of coffee and listening to the music and message. Then, on the fourth week, he moved into the seating area and responded to the invitation to surrender his life to Christ. A year later, this same man was utilizing his musical talent, playing his guitar as a member of our SNL band.

As news of SNL spread through the community, the Saturday night crowds began to grow. And with the growth came numerous changes. Each week our crowds began to look less like us. The stated goal of our staff and elders was to reach the unchurched and dechurched. But I think we didn't expect their outward appearance and actions to be so unchurchy. Some of the new attendees arrived on their Harleys and dropped their cigarette butts near the main entrance. Many of them sported tattoos in every visible area of skin, and their muscular, hairy arms depicted very unwholesome themes. And if these looked bad, the guys looked worse! (Possible a little exaggeration here)

I would be remiss if I did not clarify that SNL was not limited to the young, the restless, and rebellious. To our amazement, we had folks in their eighties attending the meetings. Some came with earplugs to dampen the volume of the music. But they loved what they were seeing: the unchurched, the dechurched, the hurting, and the broken, coming in search of life, healing, and reality. One would think that scene would have been encouraging to all of us, but it wasn't. To some on our leadership team, it was just too much change to digest. In the words of Shannon O'Dell, "Everyone likes change---except when it makes things different."[14]

"ARE YOU WILLING TO TRADE 30 OF OUR FAMILIES FOR THAT CROWD?"

In response to the format and content of Saturday Night Life, one of my dearest friends and fellow-elders came to me expressing his concern. According to him, others had expressed their displeasure with SNL, and wanted it stopped. I explained to my friend that our young staff members leading SNL were reaching a group of people that we had not been able to reach in our Sunday morning meetings. I further suggested that those who disliked SNL simply attend on Sunday mornings instead. A few days later my elder-colleague was back in my office. This time, the message was more urgent. Those opposing the Saturday night meeting did not want their tithes to be used to support SNL, and furthermore, they did not want their children to associate with the likes of those attending on Saturday night. I felt as if a dagger had been thrust into my chest. Ten years earlier, we had launched Life Center with the expressed purpose of reaching the unreached. And now that we were beginning to accomplish our mission statement, some were demanding we cease and desist.

The final showdown came a few days later when the same brother again visited my office with an ultimatum and a difficult question. The ultimatum was this: Either we stop SNL, or run the risk of losing up to thirty families from our congregation. Then came the question that absolutely stunned me. He asked "Are you willing to trade thirty of our families for that crowd?"

Although having to make the choice was extremely difficult, I knew I had no choice. Faced with that question I could only wonder WWJD? The correct answer was evident. When presented with a similar scenario and similar question Jesus responded, "I did not come to minister to the righteous, but to the unrighteous" and "those who are well do not need a physician, but those who are sick do." As my friend and brother left my office, I felt my heart would explode. We had worked side by side for years with, what I thought was a common vision. I knew he loved me and I loved him, but we were about to go separate ways. Only years later would I better understand what was taking place in my office that day.

In 2007, I was working as a chaplain with the Westminster Police Department in Westminster, California. Whenever I was riding patrol with one of our officers, I was required to wear a department uniform and a protective vest. One evening when I was getting dressed to go on duty, I retrieved my vest from the closet and proceeded to put it on. As I opened the vest I noticed a warning label I had never read. The message was as follows: "Caution: this vest is designed to repel ballistic projectiles, but may be penetrated by sharp objects." As I pondered these words, an even clearer message appeared to me. "Those who are closest to you are most likely to injure you." How many of us have found that to be true in life? We usually receive the deepest wounds from those closest to us.

My heart ached as some of my closest friends chose to leave our fellowship over our decision to continue Saturday Night Life. True to his warning, my fellow-elder and approximately thirty families left our fellowship, leaving us understaffed in most of our ministries, and reducing our monthly income by approximately $10,000. Salaries were reduced. Medical insurance was eliminated and retirement plans put on hold. It was a difficult season for all of us (the ones who stayed and the ones who left) who sincerely felt we were following our convictions and endeavoring to seek God's perfect will for our lives and our ministries. Apparently, it was the price of progress, and it was painful.

As our Saturday Night Life continued to develop, it became increasingly apparent to me that our younger staff was doing a more effective job of reaping the harvest in our area than we older leaders.

On several occasions, I had approached our younger team members to consider who might be the one to follow me as senior pastor of Life Center. Our youngest son, Steve, had been our youth pastor for nine years. With his photographic memory, a Sanguine personality, and a genuine love for God and people, Georgiann and I felt Steve might be God's choice to succeed me in the lead role. However, when I approached him with this idea, he said, "Dad, I wouldn't touch that with a twenty-foot pole."

Having grown up in a pastor's home, and having witnessed the best and the worst of church life, Steve felt confident that he was as close to pastoring as he ever desired to be. Our nephew, Jerry Shaffer, was our Missions Director with a sharp mind, a gregarious personality, and a genuine heart for God, and I wondered if he might just be the one God would choose to lead the Life Center family to reach the next generation. However, Jerry felt that God was leading him to launch a new work in Chicago Land. Still, I felt in my heart that soon God would have me step aside and pass the torch to a younger man to lead the outreach to young families in the Arkansas River Valley. So I kept praying and seeking God's will and plan.

By the end of 2001, Saturday Night Life had become a strong, vital outreach of Life Center with a distinct personality and character. In order to facilitate SNL, we had asked members of our Sunday morning meetings to serve on Saturday nights. Therefore, many of our older members were staffing our nurseries, café, children's church, audio/visual, and usher/greeter ministries. We were all busy and excited to see the new blood coming into the church. But still, I had the nagging feeling God would have me pass the leadership torch to the next generation. When I approached Steve again with the idea, he indicated he would prayerfully consider the idea. Over the next few months, I gave Steve an increasing amount of ministry responsibilities, both in the pulpit and out, and it was evident God's hand was upon him. So, I met with our church elders along with our outside Presbytery, and shared with them what I felt God was saying and where He was leading us. With their consent, I announced to the congregation that in January of 2002, I would step aside and Steve would become the senior pastor of Life Center. As the day approached, much prayer and preparation went into the transition. Members of our presbytery were invited to attend and participate in the meeting. Governor Mike Huckabee sent a video-taped message of encouragement and affirmation to Steve and Tonya. But, something much more exciting and confirming was discovered in our preparation.

Georgiann's father, George Clarke, had been our very first church elder ordained when we launched the church in 1990. Dad and Mom Clarke had served many years as pastors and foreign missionaries and were loved and deeply honored by our church family. But due to a liver disease, Dad Clarke's health deteriorated to the point that, in 1993, he went to be with the Lord. During his final days, Dad Clarke called each of his grandchildren to his side and ministered to them. Although he was physically weak, he prayed with them individually, leading some of them to salvation. And as they left his bedside, he handed each of them a mini-cassette of the patriarchal prayer he had prayed over them.

A MESSAGE FROM THE GRAVE

Ten years later, as we were making final preparations for the day of transition for Life Center, Georgiann remembered that her father had given Steve and Tonya a tape recording on his death bed. She asked Tonya about the tape. Tonya recalled that she and Steve had stored the tape in a safe place but had never listened to the recorded message. A couple of days later, Tonya brought the tape to Georgiann. When Georgiann began to listen to the message that Dad Clarke had recorded for Steve and Tonya, she began to weep. She then phoned me and said, "You must hear this tape." I was equally shocked by what Dad Clarke had recorded ten years earlier. On the first Sunday of January in 2002, we displayed Dad Clarke's picture on our projection screen, and he delivered the following message to Steve and Tonya via the tape recording:

"Steve, I want to tell you something concerning what I feel very strong about. The Lord has been so good to me in every way, and you have seen God move in wonderful ways at different times; I want you to know that God has a very definite plan for you and Tonya...very definite. It came to me this morning. And I could tell you some things that I feel so strong about, and as soon as your Daddy comes, I want him to tell me if I'm right or wrong.

51

And one of the things that I felt so strong about was the fact that your daddy is not going to be pastor of the church a great deal longer...did you know that? God has some work for him to do....very special. But, he can do it and he will do it, and in his place there's a young man who stands today holding my hand. And you're going to, one day not too far into the future, find yourself wearing the shoes of your pastor, your daddy. They're big shoes, boy!

And Tonya, remember, you are not called to sit idly by while this young man does something he feels very strongly about. You have before you a work to be done to the glory of God. Don't just do it because its a job; and don't just do it because you don't know anybody that's better than you are, because there are some pretty good teachers in that church; and you and your husband and myself....we agree that this is probably something that has been echoing down for a while and is soon going to become a milestone in your life and your parents' lives.

They must understand that the number two spot is not theirs anymore. Number one is Jesus. Number two is you and your family. So, be about the Father's business. Get right with it and don't let it be broken up by people who don't understand, Okay?"

Pausing to gather his strength, Dad Clarke continued, addressing Steve's friend, David Brady:

"David, I want you to be a witness to these thoughts and understand that this is not just something that an old man conjured up in his mind, but it is the power of God speaking, all right? And I want you to stand up if someone says...'Ah, Steve's dad had to do something and we've got to put up with Steve. They don't have to put up with nobody...God's putting up with them...and they had better stand behind, not before, but stand behind the ministry of the Spirit, and see what God will do."

Speaking again to Steve:

"There's a great work opening unto the church. And so, thanks so much for listening and for this little while of putting on tape what I feel in my heart that God would have me to write down. I can't write anymore so I have to speak. But, it will be words that will mean much to you and your wife. Don't back off! Don't back off from nothing. Stand up and be counted for God! And let them people know that there is a Spirit within the church, and God is moving and ministering as only He can. The Lord bless you!"

There was hardly a dry eye in the house as we all listened to Dad Clarke's message recorded ten years earlier, but confirming the current transition of ministry for our church. Although it was evident that God was leading the Life Center family into new territory, the transition was not easy. Again, the price of progress was expensive and painful. Although we all knew God had spoken confirmation through Dad Clarke, still it was not easily accepted for some. After all, most of our congregation had watched Steve grow up in the church. And, although he was now thirty years old and married, he was still just Steve, the pastor's mischievous son, who courted and married the little Presbyterian girl named Tonya Norris. Over the next several months, many changes took place as Steve began to develop his own team and plot the course for the church.

Among the many changes that occurred, the platform was remodeled, extra lighting was installed, the seats were rearranged and the Sunday morning meetings began to take on the personality and appearance of Saturday Night Life. Even the name of the church was changed to identify the new direction and ministry. Life Center officially became The Journey. Therefore, as the months passed, so did several of our church members. They passed, not from life, but to other churches. Although they loved Steve and Tonya, they had grown up under the ministry of Georgiann and me, and they felt they just could not make the transition. As the Journey began to take shape, and new families began to join, approximately a third of the congregation left. Consequently, Steve and his staff were forced to reduce their expenses dramatically. Again, it was a painful transition, one that can be described best by Steve, himself.

CHAPTER EIGHT

Passing the Torch

From Steve's perspective: I never wanted to be a pastor! I've never thought that it was a good thing to live in a fishbowl and have the eyes of everyone upon you! I grew up with this experience as a Pastor's Kid and believe me when I say, "Everyone's eyes are upon you, and everything you do will be scrutinized, criticized, and proclaimed from the rooftops." Moving from being a PK to a Pastor though, is like taking the fishbowl analogy and putting it on crack! I had seen what professing Christians could do to one another and to my parents over the years of living in their home and under their leadership, and I wasn't anxious to trade places. But God!!!! Evidently God had other plans and beginning in 1999, he started wrecking my world.

I was perfectly happy leading teenagers to Christ, helping them grow in maturity into Christ-like character, and growing the ministry of the church through young people. I've always said, you can catch big fish with little fish, meaning that a strong youth ministry would bring parents of those kids into the family of God, as well. My job allowed me pretty much total freedom to do what I felt was necessary, say what I felt was necessary, in any way I felt was necessary, without a board of well meaning, yet very cautious men and women, to veto anything that might be risky. Oh, and I also got to go on a lot of trips. Youth like to have fun, whether it's outside the church or inside…something that adults seem to have forgotten. I was having fun alright. Then 1999!

My Dad decided to take the staff to a conference in Cincinnati, Ohio, hosted at Cincinnati Vineyard by Steve Sjogren. It was called the "Off the Map Evangelism Conference." We were exposed to some ideas, concepts, and insights about the purpose of the Church that we had either forgotten or never fully understood. Believe me, that was about to change. They hammered home the point that the Church was the hope of the world... that Christ came to seek and save the lost and for some reason, the Church was failing in it's co-mission with Christ to accomplish that purpose.

It was no secret to us, or anyone else, that the Church was failing in that purpose, but it was also no secret that we didn't know what to do to fix the problem. Then it happened! They brought in four people to sit on some barstools on the stage. They told us that these people were what we would call lost, unsaved, heathens, unchurched. Then they began to ask them what they thought about us. Did you catch that? They asked THEM what they thought about us! Words like judgmental, hypocritical, boring, irrelevant, outdated, antiquated came up. They went on and on and on about the reasons why they didn't go to church and, for the most part, we could not disagree with how they felt about us. I won't go into all the reasons why people don't go to church because there is a myriad of books on the topic, but what I will say is that I personally had never considered those reasons, and I definitely had never asked THEM! But that experience changed me at the core.

How is the Church supposed to reach those people if we don't know those people? How are we to share Christ with those we don't share life with? How are we to lead those people when we don't begin by considering the needs, desires, likes, and languages of those people? These were questions that we felt must be answered if we were going to succeed in the mission given to us by Christ! So we began asking them. We'll walk through this process in later chapters but for now, let me just tell you that all the pain of progress was worth every minute, week, month, and year of it!

CHAPTER NINE

Missing Our Hour of Visitation

I am convinced that one of the keys to the remarkable growth of The Life Center/Journey and many other cutting-edge congregations across America is their leaders' willingness to shoot the sacred cows and ignore the criticisms and ridicule that inevitably arises when anyone dares to resist redundancy.

Invariably, when any new work is launched in a community it draws the ire of *Resistant Redundants*. Unfortunately, many church leaders become comfortable with the stability of their salaries, their retirement plans, and their status quo.

Regrettably, many churches that were founded on a burning passion for evangelism and discipleship evolve into the quagmire of redundancy once their buildings are completed, their choir robes are paid for, their ball team has won the state trophy, and the church machine has become well-lubricated. At this point, it becomes all too easy to expend our time and energy keeping the saints satisfied and forgetting that multitudes are still perishing all around us. Also at this stage of church life, some leaders tend to forget that they were the ones criticized, ridiculed, and labeled when their work was launched. Whenever and wherever this occurs, God will raise up a new man or woman with a burning passion for the hurting, the lost, and the dying outside the circles of the church establishment.

In the early seventies, Georgiann and I were serving as ministers of Youth and Music at First Assembly of God in Russellville, Arkansas. We had a thriving youth group and an award-winning youth choir that enjoyed the excitement of traveling throughout the region ministering to other church groups and conventions. At this time, First Assembly had long since overcome the label of "Holy Rollers", and had become one of the largest congregations in the community with enviable social status. Indeed, it was recognized that if one wanted to be elected to political office in the city or county, he or she should join First Baptist, First Methodist, or First Assembly.

As church leaders, and as a congregation, we were proud of our status. We had successfully evolved from the outcast to the in-crowd. In the foyer of our main building our trophy cases were filled with "First Place" recognition in missions, softball, Bible Quiz, and Teen Talent. Our pews were filled with saved, sanctified, and satisfied saints. And in my mind, I wondered why all the other churches didn't just close their doors and join us. Then God began to rock our boat.

Some of the college students in our youth group began attending a Bible-Study on the campus of Arkansas Tech University with a group calling themselves *The Fellowship of Christians*. Each week the students met to pray, study the Bible, and sing contemporary songs or choruses taken straight from the Bible.

I attended several of the meetings in spite of being cautioned by several of our church leaders. I found the meetings to be very informal and casual, but graced with a spiritual anointing that I personally hungered for. I was pleasantly surprised by their apparent hunger for true worship and for God's presence, and I began to look forward to their weekly gatherings. However, I must admit these bold new young lions challenged our sense of piety and order when they showed up at our church meetings with their bare feet, long hair, and totally nonreligious attitudes.

Like most other denominational leaders in our city, I did not fully embrace the motley crew who called themselves *The Fellowship of Christians*. After all, how could this group really possess God's favor and anointing when they dared to show up at the "House of God" on "The Lord's Day", wearing tattered jeans and sandals or, worse yet, barefoot? And to make matters worse, most of them had forsaken the authorized King James Version of the Bible for more questionable modern versions. After all, if the KJV was good enough for the Apostle Paul, it should be good enough for us! (Pardon the satire)

Sadly, we like many of the demoninational [15]churches of the seventies, missed a grand opportunity to embrace a fresh move of God's Spirit and drove away many of these young seekers. These new radicals calling themselves the *"Fellowship of Christians"* were branded a cult! However, we had forgotten that First Assembly of God was considered a cult when it began seven decades earlier. Life Center was branded a cult when we launched it in 1990. And you will likely be considered a cult if and when you dare to challenge the status quo spirit and break the curse of redundancy.

One can only wonder what would have happened in our established traditional churches if we had possessed enough discernment to embrace those young lions, and had recognized and addressed the crippling spirit of redundancy in our own religious circles. We need only look as far as Calvary Chapel and its founder, Chuck Smith, to answer that question.

Thank God, numerous members of the Fellowship of Christians on the campus of Arkansas Tech University were not dissuaded by the Pharisaism and religiosity of many of us who were lost in our own circles of redundancy in the Seventies. Basically shunned or ignored by the religious establishment in our city, the Fellowship of Christians endured the ridicule and insults and pressed on in their pursuit of God. Consequently, forty years later, Wayne Drain, one of the original FOC students, continues to lead the Fellowship of Christians with an international ministry impact from their modern facilities located on Interstate 40 in Russellville, Arkansas.

CHAPTER TEN

Entropic Churches

E ntropy is the Second Law of Thermodynamics. That law states that in all energy exchanges, if no energy enters or leaves the system, the potential energy of the state will always be less than that of the initial state. Many in today's world have never seen a wristwatch driven by a mainspring. At the risk of revealing my age, I will inform you that as a teenager I had to wind my watch at least every other day or it would stop running. Why? Because a spring-driven watch will run until the potential energy in the spring is expended, and not again until energy is reapplied to the spring to rewind it. Likewise, an automobile that runs out of gas will not operate again until someone adds more fuel. This law also teaches us that the flow of energy maintains order and life.

Entropy wins when organisms cease to take in energy and die. Incidentally, many of the Swiss watch makers that once were household names, no longer exist because they simply could not make the transition from winding power to batteries. Entropy developed and progress left them behind.

It is no coincidence that the Apostle Paul advised the Church to "keep on being filled with the Spirit", and to continue the process of "renewing the mind." Without that constant refilling and renewing, entropy inevitably drains the life and energy out of the believer individually and thus, the Church corporately.

The British scientist and author C.P. Snow had an excellent way of remembering the three laws of entropy:

1. You cannot win (that is, you cannot get something for nothing because matter and energy are conserved).

2. You cannot break even (you cannot return to the same energy state because there is always an increase in disorder; entropy always increases).

3. You cannot get out of the game (because absolute zero is unattainable).

This law also predicts that the entropy of an isolated system always increases with time. Entropy is the measure of the disorder or randomness of entropy and matter in a system.

Now catch that! Any organism or system that becomes isolated invites the cancer of entropy. This is why I have contended for many years that pastors and congregations should never allow themselves to become independent. Independence suggests the need of no one else, and that defies the very meaning and mission of the Church.

According to Paul's first letter to the Church in Corinth, "the eye cannot say to the hand I have no need of you, or the head to the feet, I don't need you...but rather you are all members of one body" (1 Cor. 12:21). Therefore pastors, we really do need each other regardless of our differences of opinion on worship styles, church government, and eschatology.

Who knows what could happen if Christian leaders would set aside their pride, prejudice, and preferences and network with other leaders for fellowship, prayer, and outreach? For an inspiring response to that question, ask the pastors in Almolonga, Guatemala, whose unified efforts in the mid-seventies led to such revival that the area jails were closed for lack of prisoners, and even the infertile soil became a breadbasket for their nation. (See Transformation by George Otis)

Because of the second law of thermodynamics, both energy and matter in the Universe are becoming less useful as time goes on. We are informed by the intelligentsia of our day that perfect order occurred in the instant after the Big Bang when energy and matter and all of the forces of the Universe were unified. What a powerful, yet strange observation made by educated fools created by the God whose existence they deny (Psalm 14:1).

I know of few things more discouraging to a pastor than trying to lead a group that has become entropic, stagnant, and unproductive. Those who set their heels in the sand and refuse to move forward become a hindrance to themselves and everyone around them. I think Charles Spurgeon addressed this subject more powerfully than anyone I've studied. Note his lecture written July 26, 1874:

"It is harder a great deal to work for Jesus with a church which is lukewarm than it would be to begin without a church. Give me a dozen earnest spirits and put me down anywhere in London, and by God's good help we will soon cause the wilderness and the solitary place to rejoice; but give me the whole lot of you, half-hearted, undecided, and unconcerned, what can I do? You will only be a drag upon a man's zeal and earnestness. Five thousand members of a church all lukewarm will be five thousand impediments, but a dozen earnest, passionate spirits, determined that Christ shall be glorified and souls won, must be more than conquerors; in their very weakness and fewness will reside capacities for being the more largely blessed of God. Better nothing than lukewarmness."

Fellow-leaders, are we open to a fresh infilling of the Spirit of God? Are we open to the transitions required of us to keep us fresh and relevant? Are we open to the encouragement, enlightenment, reproof, and counsel of others outside our circles, or have we become so closed in our religious systems that we are becoming entropic, and thus redundant?

DÉJÀ VU

A short time ago, Georgiann and I visited a church near where I was born. This church is one of the oldest in its denomination and has a rich heritage of revivals and strong witness in the community. It is now led by a very conscientious man whom I consider to be a personal friend and brother. As we sat in the church meeting on Sunday morning, Georgiann and I both experienced déjà vu as the worship leader led the congregation in songs from our

61

childhood...songs like *"When We All Get to Heaven"* and *"Love Lifted Me."* My friend delivered a moving message to approximately forty people. My heart ached as he poured out his soul and lamented that, without a change of direction, their local church could easily cease to exist in a few years. With tears in his eyes, he chided the congregation over the fact that approximately half a dozen people now attend Wednesday night meetings with scarcely few more on Sunday nights.

As I listened to my friend pour out his heart of concern, I could not hold back the tears. I reflected back on the great revival meetings that impacted my life as a child, and I tried to calculate the dozens of young men and women who had surrendered their lives to full-time ministry there over the past eighty years. But I think I wept equally for my burdened pastor-friend who, perhaps unconsciously, held the keys to changes necessary to reverse the entropic redundancy and prevent the death of the church. But change is seldom easy, and is often costly. Change often costs us our sense of security, our preferences, our status quo, our reputation, and even our friends.

Sadly, as I reflect on my friend's sermon and his heart-felt challenge to his congregation, I can fairly accurately predict the future of his ministry. He has several choices: He will continue to coddle the spirit of status quo and pray, prepare, and preach to a small handful of saved and satisfied saints; He will become weary in well-doing and leave the pastoral ministry; In discouragement, he will resign from the position he is now serving and will move on to lead another congregation, only to face the same spirit of redundancy in a different location with different faces; or he will prayerfully, and courageously, bite the bullet, discover and expose entropy, break the curse of redundancy, and lead the congregation into new vistas of Kingdom advancement. Unfortunately for the pastor, this will probably require butchering, barbequing, and serving a truckload of religious cows at the next church supper.

CHAPTER ELEVEN

Endowed and Redundant

W hile serving in our first pastorate in Lakewood, California in the Seventies and Eighties, life was never dull. Our family was young, and our church was bustling with growth. In a span of thirteen years, our congregation had grown from slightly over one hundred members to over eight hundred. However, due to the fact that our building was landlocked on less than an acre with fewer than thirty five parking spaces, providing seating and parking for our expanding congregation was a constant challenge and dilemma for me. To add to my frustration was the fact that within five miles of our facility were half a dozen spacious church facilities that housed less than fifty worshipers on any given weekend. Most of these were traditional mainline churches that had, long ago, lost their vision, their enthusiasm, and their younger members. What remained of once vibrant churches were now just shells containing a few elderly members and maintained by substantial endowment funds.

As the years passed and we continued to add meeting times to our weekend schedules, I repeatedly made contact with leaders of the churches in our area to inquire if we could rent space, purchase, or even trade facilities to accommodate our ever-growing congregation. Each time, I came away disappointed. For though some of these facilities could accommodate up to a thousand people, the fact that less than fifty members remained was of little concern to the leaders. Thanks to their church endowment funds, their mortgages and utilities were paid, and their salaries, retirement funds, and vacation packages were all secure. Therefore, the fact that a church a few blocks away was reaching hundreds of lost souls in grossly inadequate facilities was of no concern to those who appeared to be redeemed, but redundant.

Sadly, this scenario continues to be repeated all across our nation, where courageous young leaders are challenging the status quo of religion and tearing down strongholds of evil right in the shadows of redundant religious institutions. Therefore, I keep asking why, for the sake of eternal souls, don't many of the redeemed redundant, saved, sanctified, and satisfied church leaders either retire and move to Leisure World, or trade, share, sell or donate their facilities to churches actually carrying out the Great Commission? Thankfully, I am not the only voice pressing this issue today.

EVIDENCE THE CURSE IS BROKEN

How can we determine if the curse of redundancy is broken in our lives and in our churches? I believe the answer is found in the answer to another question: *Do we love the eternal souls of men, women, boys and girls more than we cherish the temporal benefits of man's approval, creature comforts, and retirement plans?* If the answer to the latter question is yes, we will pay whatever price for true progress and the cycle of redundancy will be broken. We all have choices to make in life. And it seems the older we become, the more likely we are to become trapped in our comfort zones, fearful to make dramatic changes, lest we jeopardize our temporal security.

PERSONAL THOUGHTS ON THE PRICE OF PROGRESS

Many have asked me what it is like to step aside and pass the torch to a younger leader prior to retirement age. Others have asked me how I'm enjoying retirement. Let me set the record straight. First of all, I do not believe retirement should be in the vocabulary of any child of God. For as long as we are breathing, we have a responsibility to preach the good news, wherever, whenever, and however possible.

Frankly, stepping aside from more than thirty years of full-time pulpit ministry has been one of the most difficult challenges of my life. At the same time, it has been, and continues to be, one of the most rewarding seasons of my life. So for the sake of those of you who are struggling with the price of progress, let me share both the positive and negative aspects, along with a few recommendations to make your transition more rewarding.

Be prepared to remove yourself from your local church for a season. It can be extremely difficult for a congregation to attach to a new leader while the previous leader continues to sit on the front row. Those who have been converted and discipled under your ministry may find it difficult to follow the direction of a new leader. So be open to other avenues of ministry outside your local church and possibly outside of your locale. Shortly after Steve assumed my role as senior pastor, Georgiann and I served a four-year mission in California, allowing Steve time to spread his wings and develop his own style, free from the constant stare and critique of his parents.

Be open to the development of para-church ministries that will help strengthen the local church, and will continue to fulfill your passion to reach and care of hurting people. For me personally, those para-church ministries consist of the following:

A. H.E.L.P.

Hands Extending Love and Provision is a community outreach I developed to minister to the practical needs of wounded veterans, widows, single parents, and others in need of wheelchair ramps or home repairs they cannot afford to pay for. Although I am not personally skilled in construction, we have many in our congregation who are. So when a need in our community is brought to my attention, we have a team of electricians, plumbers, roofers, and carpenters who are ready and willing to take our fully-equipped trailer to the site where we share the love of Jesus in practical ways.

B. POLICE CHAPLAINCY

While assisting with the restoration of a church in Westminster, California in 2005, I was invited to become a chaplain for the Westminster Police Department. This required extensive training with the other chaplains and with the department personnel, and required me to ride patrol with the officers on a regular basis. This opened a whole new world of ministry for me and provided an insight into a world that few pastors and church members will ever see. For not only was I allowed into a distinct and close fraternity with a divorce rate near one hundred percent, but I was also exposed to the real world of crime, drugs, gangs, domestic violence, homelessness, and poverty that few church leaders witness. My love and compassion for the officers and their families, and my desire to penetrate and touch the unchurched/dechurched in our society, led me to seek and obtain certification as an International Police Chaplain. When Georgiann and I relocated to Arkansas in 2007, I connected with the Pope County Sheriff's Office and now serve as a Chaplain for that department. Further, the certification with the International Conference of Police Chaplains has opened doors for me with Law Enforcement agencies and personnel around the world.

CHAPTER TWELVE

Breaking the Rurals

I chose the title of this chapter after reading Shannon O'dell's great book on *Transforming Church in Rural America*. What Shannon and his dedicated team have done in a small town in Arkansas is nothing short of miraculous, and is living proof that great churches can be built wherever individuals are willing to pay the price of progress and break the curse of redundancy. Their willingness to listen to God's directives and follow them without compromise is an encouragement and challenge to anyone who desires to be effective in expanding the Kingdom of God.

In October 2002, Southside Baptist Church in Lead Hill, Arkansas had thirty one members. At the same time, Shannon O'Dell was serving as pastor to students at First Southern Baptist Church in Del City, Oklahoma. For some time, Shannon had sensed that God was calling him to pastor a church that would engage culture and replicate the Acts 2 church. But never in his wildest dreams did he think God would call him to start with a dying congregation in rural Arkansas. Therefore, he was extremely reluctant to reply when someone from the Arkansas congregation asked him to consider becoming their pastor. The idea of moving his family from the Metroplex to the boonies was simply unthinkable, but God's idea of progress is not always reasonable. After much discussion and prayer, and against the advice of many of his closest friends and colleagues, Shannon moved his family to a small town in Northern Arkansas, and the results of that move have been incredible. Sensing that God wanted to do something brand new in that region, they renamed the church Brand New Church. And, brand new is an understatement!

By 2005, the church had outgrown two campuses and needed more space. Since the O'Dells moved to Arkansas, the 31-member Lead Hill congregation has exploded to over one thousand, and has expanded into nine towns in northern Arkansas. The ministry is now based in Bergman, a town with a population of 407. In December 2006, BNC averaged more than 1,000 people in attendance each week, with O'Dell estimating that about 60 percent drive from the larger city of Harrison. Others drive from smaller cities like Yellville, Lead Hill, Pindall, and Kingston. According to O'Dell, "When church is done right, they'll drive from anywhere. But it's not about the numbers. It's about changed lives, about marriages and families being put back together, and drug addicts being set free. And it's about a congregation passionate about being biblical in their structure and ministry." [16]

Someone might look at Brand New Church and Shannon O'Dell with envy for what appears to be an overnight success. But reading their story will reveal the real story of personal sacrifice and rejection, and enduring the criticism, lies, and vitriolic actions of those who favored redundancy over relevance.

Anyone who envisions transforming a redundant organization into a vital living Church must face the reality that it will not be easy. It will be difficult. It will be wrought with much pain, patience, and endurance. But the product is worth the price! Nothing is more rewarding than seeing hungry, thirsty souls finding the Bread of Life and the Living Water.

Shannon O'Dell and his team challenged, confronted, and defeated the spirit of religion and redundancy in a rural area of Northwest Arkansas. As I mentioned earlier, part of their strategy was renaming the new rural church *"Brand New Church."* I personally believe any congregation that is a true Church will remain in a state of constant renewal. For when it ceases to become new, it will become redundant!

For the sake of the Kingdom of God and reaching those Jesus died for, are you willing to alter your preferences and opinions about the church methodology? A Gaelic proverb states, "Nothing is easy for the unwilling." And if you are unwilling to face your fears and emotions, then forward progress on improving your quality of life will not be easy.

In the closing session of Catalyst 2008, Andy Stanley delivered five quotes that he and his staff at Northpoint Church in Atlanta, Georgia, work with on a daily basis.

"To reach people no one else is reaching, we must do things no one else is doing." Craig Groeschel

On this point, Andy reminded the church leaders that there are people who will never step through the doors of our churches, no matter how cool our churches are. So how will we reach them? We have to think of brand new ways of going to them, even if "traditional church people" don't necessarily like them.

My personal experience has revealed that many traditional church people will not merely "not necessarily like" the changes. Operating under the same demonic religious spirit that motivated the Pharisees of Jesus' day, some will violently oppose change! When this occurs, visionary leaders must keep their eyes on the goal of reaching those Jesus died for.

I think I'll never forget the reaction in our city when our Pastor/son, Steve, rented a billboard across from WalMart and publicized the message: "You don't have to believe to belong! THE JOURNEY". Wow, the critics went ballistic! Phone lines jammed, our emails were flooded, and "Letters to the editor" centered around the audacity, and perhaps blasphemy, of the Journey and its pastor. And true to form, the loudest, most vitriolic criticism came from the religious crowd, professing Christians, and church members from our area. In an effort to stem the tide of criticism, Steve wrote an article for the local newspaper clarifying that the billboard message was relational, not theological. Being the radical church leader that he is, Steve possessed the crazy notion that Jesus really meant we can come "Just as we are", and He will change us. The radical billboard message accomplished two beneficial things in our city:

It gave the local Pharisees new fodder to chew, thereby diverting, for a season, their criticism for other pastors in our city. It provided The Journey with loads of free press, and drew scores of visitors to check us out. (Many came because they didn't have to believe to belong. And we are grateful that many stayed, belonged, and now believe!)

According to Andy Stanley, "Some people won't donate more money for church operational costs, but they will donate money to try something radically new to reach people no one has reached." So our goal must be to "become preoccupied with who you haven't reached as opposed to those you want to keep."

This is never easy, for it will often require leaders to part company with close friends and associates who began the journey with you, but cannot, or will not make the adjustments necessary to move the next level of church development.

"The next generation product almost never comes from the previous generation." Al Reis

On this point, Andy gave the following advice: "If you are 45 or older, the next great idea most likely won't come from you. Your job, instead, is to constantly seek out the next generation and hear what they are thinking. Enable their visions to come true. Go look to the 20 year olds. If you want to find examples of radically different thinking, you should be paying attention to what your Student Ministries guys are talking about.

Don't do to the next generation what was done to yours. Don't say, 'We don't do things like that.' Stop and think about what they are proposing. Give them space, money, social capital, and the freedom to fail."

In our stage of church development in Arkansas, as the senior leader, I had to face the truth of that statement and adjust accordingly. I had to face the fact that in our city, in the middle of the Bible Belt, with dozens of full-Gospel churches, most all of them were led by leaders over age fifty. And few, if any of them, were effectively reaching the 65% of area residents under 35 years old.

"What do I believe is impossible to do in my field...but if it could be done would fundamentally change my business?" Future Edge/The Paradigm Book, Joel Barker

On this subject, Andy informed more than 10,000 young church leaders that one of the stickiest problems in the previous generation of church leadership and growth was requiring a great leader to also be a great communicator. "Those are two skills, and not that many people have both. What if a church leader didn't have to beat the brunt of communicating?"

At Northpoint Church, the leader/communicator issue was solved by the multi-site video venue. Utilizing this venue, a teaching pastor can communicate well, while each campus can be led by a great leader. This fundamentally changed church growth. It did the same for us at the Journey, in Arkansas.

When we outgrew our present facilities, hard choices had to be made. Here is how Steve Pyle describes the dilemma: "In 2011, we were again out of space. With an auditorium that would seat 400, we were operating a Saturday night meeting and two Sunday morning meetings. In spite of the multi-service schedule, our auditorium, our nurseries, and our parking lots were maxed out. The idea of borrowing money to build larger facilities was not feasible due to the struggling economy. And to further complicate matters, we had more than 100 people driving 25-40 miles to attend our meetings with fuel prices at an all-time high. After much prayer, the decision was made to launch a new video site, twenty-five miles to the West with a local campus pastor. This has proven not only to be a good idea, but a God idea."

In 2010, no other church in our area had attempted the multi-campus venue. But as the late, great Zig Ziglar reminded us, "If you want to be successful, find out what everyone is doing, then don't do that!" In other words, be courageous enough to break the rules!

Andy Stanley proposed: "If we got kicked out and the board brought in a new CEO, what would he do? Why shouldn't we walk out the door, come back in, and do it ourselves?"

"Only the Paranoid Survive"
Andy Grove

On this point, Andy reminded the audience: "The first thing an outsider might say about your organization is 'Why in the world are you doing that?' We fall in love with the way we do things and forget to constantly reevaluate. The fact of life is that usually without pain, there is no gain. And usually that pain is financial.

Where are we manufacturing energy? These are the programs that we do because we do. We aren't all that excited about them, but it is what we do. We just manufacture energy. Get rid of them.

It is painful to change. Yes, your context makes it difficult to get rid of this program, or that. It is difficult everywhere. It always hurts."

Did you catch that last sentence? "It always hurts!" Not sometimes, in some places, with some people. Change always hurts. Change disrupts our comfort zones and our preferences; Change often wounds the pride of those who pioneered a program, developed it, and possibly kept it on life support for the past decade. So the question for all of us who are charged with the responsibility of leading the Church is not whether making changes will be painful, but how much more painful and destructive will be the result if we refuse to make changes.

"When your memories exceed your dreams, the end is near."
Michael Hammer

On this final point, Andy emphasized: "We don't want to be an expert on the previous generation! Celebrate the past, yes, but don't be so celebratory that you forget the future. Are you willing to be invested in the future? Complacency breeds failure."

My earnest prayer is that every reader and every leader will digest this truth. Although this is critical to the life of any organization, it is urgent that every church leader and every church member hear this and live this. Time is too short and our world is too sick for us to live in the past. Yes, many of us in the Church today know because *He Touched Me, I'll Fly Away* to my *Mansion over the Hilltop*, where *Everybody Will Be Happy Over There, When We All Get to Heaven* and *They Ring Those Golden Bells for You and Me*. However, we must also be aware there are those around us who regret that *All Their Exes Live in Texas;* They've heard *Hell's Bells*, and are searching for a *Stairway to Heaven;* and because *There's a Hole in the World Tonight*, they *Still Haven't Found What They're Looking For*; and some of them want to know *What's Love Got to Do With It?* Still others feel they are *Locked Out of Heaven*, they might *Die Young,* or *Anything Could Happen.*

The bottom line is the fact that styles and preferences change with time and cultures, but one thing remains constant. Jesus Christ came to love and rescue every human from hopelessness, death, and destruction, and somehow, we must find the ways and means to connect His love with those searching for it.

CHAPTER THIRTEEN

Sacrificing Sacred Cows

My question for pastors and church members is this: What are you willing to sacrifice to reach the unconverted in your area? I certainly don't claim to have all the answers to reaching our world for the Kingdom of God. But having served as a pastor for more than thirty years, and having observed the changes in society around us, I believe I can say without successful contradiction, that the new generation will not be reached with the old methods.

For the traditional church in America the facts are sobering: We are living among people who do not speak our language, do not hear as we hear, and do not share our values? We cannot, and must not, change our message of the Good News of a living/loving God for a dying world. The message of the Church is not negotiable, but the methods are!

Having been there, done that, bought a trailer load of T-shirts, and proudly bear the scars of the churchianity battles, let me mention just a few of the sacred cows that may have to sacrificed for the sake of winning the lost. And due to the fact that the changes required of you will demand blood, sweat, and tears, let me present this in a humorous form. For if you choose change over redundancy, I can assure you of the need of regular seasons of laughter in the days to come.

Since many of us are well acquainted with all-church "pot-luck" dinners, let me suggest some menu items for any church willing to change:

MARINATED MEMORIALS

What are these? If you've been around church for many years you've seen them! You will find them attached to the ends of pews. Small brass plates are attached with tiny brads as a reminder to all who pass this way that this pew was donated in memory of Grandpa Johnson or Grandma Smith. Or you may find it attached to the Hammond Organ purchased in memory of Deacon Jones who taught the fifth grade boys faithfully for thirty years. Or yet still, you may view this memorial each time you witness a baptism service and gaze at the image of Jesus looking down approvingly from the beautiful stained glass window donated fifty years ago by the family of the brother who donated the land for the church facilities. Oh what heavenly memories these memorials recapture in the minds of your saintly congregants! And oh what hellish responses are in store for you the day you mention replacing the pews with stackable chairs to create a multi-purpose facility. And perish the thought of removing the stained glass window to install your new media screen! I can assure you that scores of churches have split over lesser issues.

SAUTEED SCHEDULES

There is hardly a more sacred day on the church schedule than Sunday. After all, most of us were taught from our youth that Sunday is "The Lord's Day!" (I assume the other days are ours!) And the mere mention of "having church" on a day other than Sunday is sure to kindle the righteous indignation of many of the saints. And Sunday School on Saturday is obviously an oxymoron! However, for the sake of reaching the lost, many leaders will find it necessary to adjust your schedules to meet those of the culture and demographics around you.

What if you are in a situation and an area where there are no buildings available on Sunday? What if your present facility can no longer accommodate your congregation on Sunday? Are you willing to sacrifice the day for the harvest? If you are, you can be assured of criticism from some of your peers and some in your pews. And when this happens, just try to keep in mind, these same critics probably grew up singing the great old hymn titled, "Ain't It A Shame?" Let me explain:

Some time ago, Georgiann and I were in Atlanta, Texas, visiting my father in the Golden Villa Nursing Home. At age one hundred, Dad loved to go to the fellowship center where I would play the piano and we would sing old Gospel favorites. On our recent visit there, I was thumbing through one of the many hymnals various visitors have donated to the center, when I came across the most unusual song I have ever seen published. I trust you will be as "touched" as I when I read the lyrics:

Ain't It A Shame

Ain't it a shame to work on Sunday
Ain't it a shame, a working shame.
Ain't it a shame to work on Sunday,
Ain't it a shame, a working shame.
Ain't it a shame to work on Sunday.
When you got Monday, Tuesday, and Wednesday,
and you got Thursday, Friday, and Saturday, Ain't it a shame.

Ain't it a shame to joyride on Sunday, Ain't it a shame?
Ain't it a shame to joyride on Sunday, Ain't it a shame?

When you've got Monday, Tuesday, Wednesday, Thursday, Friday,
Saturday, Ain't it a shame to joyride on Sunday, Ain't it a shame?

Ain't it a shame to lie on Sunday, Ain't it a shame?
Ain't it a shame to lie on Sunday, Ain't it a shame?

When you've got Monday, Tuesday, Wednesday, Thursday, Friday,
Saturday, ain't it shame to lie on Sunday, Ain't it a shame?

Ain't it a shame to gossip on Sunday, ain't it a shame?
Ain't it a shame to gossip on Sunday, ain't it a shame?

When you've got Monday, Tuesday, Wednesday, Thursday, Friday, Saturday, Ain't it a shame to gossip on Sunday Ain't it a shame?

Strange as it may seem, this classic was published in the 1956 Heavenly Highway Hymnbook which was a Stamps-Baxter Publication. Stranger still is the probability that congregations during that time period sang this song with passion. Tragically, many professing Christians seem to live those lyrics! As I wrote in *Stop GOING to Church*, the practice of GOING to church on Sunday, rather than BEING the Church 24/7, has produced an epidemic of hypocrisy that has repelled countless seekers. No wonder Ghandi was quoted as commenting on the Christians of his day, "I like your Christ, but I do not like your Christians."

THE CASSEROLE

What would a church Pot Luck or "Dinner on the Ground" be without those delicious casseroles? Rather than take the time to seek out and shoot the cows individually, let's just throw a bunch of them in the pot and prepare a casserole. Although this may not fit every church, it should provide a menu to serve many of your present and future needs for change. Following are a few of the ingredients we have found necessary to include in our casseroles for the sake of growing the church and expanding the Kingdom:

1. Sunday night meetings. Oh, I know this is a precious one, so dear to our hearts. Seriously, I, like many of you, had my life transformed in great Sunday evening meetings. However, schedules must never take precedent over mission.

Now, before you start ripping out pages, sending me emails, and de-friending me on Facebook, let me hasten to say, I'm not suggesting you cancel your Sunday evening meetings just for the sake of change. However, once your congregation outgrows your present facility, you may find it necessary to find multiple uses for your auditorium, such as youth meetings, marriage seminars, etc. And once you are forced to add multiple weekend services, you will find it quite difficult to persuade your ministry teams who work multiple services on Sunday morning, to return Sunday evening to repeat the process for a group of believers who attended at least one of the meetings on Sunday morning. And leaders, prepare yourself prayerfully and skillfully when you sacrifice this most sacred cow.

Experience has shown it is advisable not to make this transition suddenly, but with much prayer, planning, and prudence. When multiple services and limited facilities pressed us to transition, we planned Sunday evening community outreaches, fellowship experiences in homes, and other functions that did not require the services of an already very busy pastoral team. Presently, our Sunday evenings are used for home group meetings, elective classes, and (perish the thought) just relaxing with family members, friends, and neighbors.

2. Verbal Announcements: I realize Deacon Jones has faithfully given the announcements for the past thirty years, and he's so good at recognizing those celebrating birthdays, and leading us in that stirring anthem of "Oh Happy Birthday." But we no longer have thirty in the congregation. We now have three hundred, or five hundred, or one thousand. So shoot the cow and purchase a computer and projector to display the pertinent upcoming events. I guarantee you will preserve valuable time in your meetings and will capture the attention of attendees who will otherwise tune you out after the second verbal announcement. And remember, when you're purchasing the new equipment, don't forget to order a nice plaque to honor Deacon Jones for his thirty years of service. He might even stay! If he does, offer him training on the computer!

3. Hymnals: More than a few church relationships have been strained over the subject of removing the hymnals and replacing them with computer-driven lyrics displayed with high resolution projectors on walls or screens. However, distressed saints, consider the advantages:

A. Reduced costs in the church budget

B. Your hands are free to express your praise to God.

C. Your eyes are no longer trained on a book, but you are looking upward!

D. No time is wasted trying to locate the correct page number.

E. Any hymn, chorus, or anthem desired is instantly available at the touch of a button.

Space is not adequate to include all the items we have included in our casseroles. However, I trust you get the message. If it no longer serves your vision and the Great Commission, stop it!

So be prepared for battle, brave warrior! Are you willing to pay the price of progress? Did God call you to be a pastor or a pacifier? And tenured board member or senior saint, are you willing to sacrifice your preferences, opinions, and traditions for sake of reaching the lost souls around you? If not, you may succeed in winning the earthly debate you're sure to engage in, and you may even succeed in doing things your way, but while you're at it, pray that God spares you the experience of facing the perished souls you could have reached were you willing to barbeque your favorite cow!

CHAPTER FOURTEEN

Suited For Ministry

T he casual atmosphere of contemporary church meetings in the United States has created abundant fodder for internet bloggers and theological debaters. A new generation of church leaders has arisen that cares little about traditional dress codes. Consequently, it is not uncommon today to see well-known church leaders addressing congregations while dressed in jeans and open collars, often to the chagrin, criticism, and perhaps envy of clerical-robed, and suit and tied ecclesiastical leaders. I must admit that I struggle with determining where casual ends and laziness begins. For instance, does our desire to be contemporary/casual permit us to pull wrinkled clothing from the hamper, jump into our soiled Nikes, and rush to the pulpit to deliver the Good News? As I struggle to find the balance, I recall that I'm of a generation that turned people away from public worship because we determined they were improperly dressed to enter "God's House" to "visit the King."

I'm ashamed to admit that in my earlier years of ministry I admonished the church to wear their "Sunday Best" when coming to "God's House" to "Meet the King." When God challenged me to prepare and write *"Stop GOING to Church,"* He radically shook my religious house by reminding me that we believers ARE the *House of God* and we live with the King 24/7.

To believe otherwise is to limit our understanding of the house of God to the Old Testament where God's people had to literally go to the tabernacle, or the temple, to visit with God. Therefore, to believe that we visit the King on Sundays is to severely limit our communion and intimacy with the very One who desires daily interaction with us.

Unfortunately, confusion over the identity of the House of God still creates great misunderstanding in and through the Church today, as evidenced through the following testimonials and articles: In 2008, a young lady posted her complaint on City-Data Forum, an Internet forum on Religion and Spirituality. She shared her frustration with the world as follows:

"I used to go a local UPC church. Well one of my best friends still goes there. She is on the cleaning staff. She's been having back problems and asked if I'd go help her clean this past Saturday. So I did. I went in black capri pants and a Tinkerbell shirt. Not trashy, pants weren't tight or low cut, shirt was not overly tight....Well the pastor's wife walked by me, stopped, looked at me. I said Hi with a big smile ready to greet her politely, and she turned and kept walking without a word. I thought it was my imagination, but it turns out that she talked to my friend and told her that if I come to help her again, that I "know their doctrine on clothes and shouldn't disrespect the house of God by wearing pants"....I must say that I was rather upset for awhile. I never would have thought she'd be like that. I find this behavior not to be that of a UPC pastor's wife, but of someone who is really stuck up and arrogant."

Now, consider the following excerpts from an article written by Dr. Karen Pansler-Lam and posted on Libertyadvocate.com, titled, *"No Reverence in God's House."* As we examine this article, I ask the reader to note how many references are made to the "House of God", "God's House", and "The Sanctuary."

In this article, Dr. Pansler-Lam compares attending a state dinner at the White House with church attendance by posing the following question: "If we were invited to a state dinner at the White House, naturally we would wear our best clothes to the President's house. Right? Why do we casually wear whatever makes us *feel comfortable* when we are invited to God's house? Why do professing Christians show disrespect for God's house by wearing casual clothes, and make no proper physical or spiritual preparation to *come and dine* with the Lord? Many people today – both young and old – don't feel like dressing with respect to worship in the house of God. Today, there is no respect for the House of God. But this was not always so. . ."

The writer then quotes from several books on etiquette. Quoting from *the 1882 Edition of American Etiquette and Rules of Politeness,* she writes, "The congregation who build a church, build it and continue to regard it as the house of God. It is then a place where the greatest deference, respect and reverence are due."

I challenge the reader to compare this quote with the words of the apostle Paul who wrote to the church in Corinth: "Do you not know that you are the temple of God?" and "do you not know that your body is the temple of the Holy Spirit who is in you?" (1 Corinthians 3:16)

Dr. Pansler-Lam goes on to quote from *The Standard Book of Etiquette,* by Lillian Eichler Watson: "We go to church to join with others in prayer, to offer thanks for our blessings, and to ask for help in knowing and doing the things that are right. Your church is God's house, so it's natural to approach it in a spirit of reverence and a worshipful mood."

According to Lillian Eichler, "Your church is God's house." According to the Apostle, Paul, "You are God's house." I wonder whom should we believe?

Quoting from *Manners to Grow On: How-To-Do Book for Boys and Girls,* Dr. Pansler-Lam writes: "On the Sabbath, and especially for communion, a man should approach the altar in coat and tie. He may come and go to the church in his shirt sleeves if that is the custom of his group and the weather is intolerable, but certainly he must maintain the utmost dignity in church." (Too bad for the guys who don't own suits and ties)

The writer of the Liberty Advocate article goes on to quote from Eleanor Boykin's 1940 edition of *This Way, Please: A book of Manners,* Amy Vanderbilt's *Everyday Etiquette,* 1968, and *The New Emily Post's Etiquette,* 1975, all of which equated and confused the place of worship with the Church, which according to the New Testament epistles is clearly a people, not a place.

In chapter three of *Stop GOING to Church*, under the section on *Desecrating the Sanctuary*, I attempted to illustrate the absurdity of equating the Church and the Sanctuary with the meeting place:

"Let me suggest that your pastor schedule and announce a 'casual day' for your local church service next Sunday morning. Dress will be casual. Popcorn and soft drinks will be served. (Beer and wine permissible only if you BYOB) A large-screen television set will be placed on the communion table and the congregation will be treated to a rerun of NYPD Blue, Silk Stockings, or The Howard Stern Show.....Did I detect a gasp by the reader? Are you shocked or offended that I would suggest such activity in the church? Why? The answer I most often receive is "It would be disrespectful and irreverent in the sanctuary!" Oh would it really? The truth is this occurs in the Church every week. But the disrespect for the sanctuary occurs when church members subject their minds to such trash in the privacy of their homes. Remember, we don't GATHER in the sanctuary, we LIVE in the sanctuary. The Apostle Paul wrote in 1 Corinthians 3:16, "Don't you know that you yourselves are God's temple and that God's Spirit dwells in your midst?" (NIV)

So if we the people are the Church, and we are individual sanctuaries, then who gets to decide the proper dress code for ministers...the Pope, Denominational leaders, or local pastors? Can we settle this question here and now and stop the quarrelling? Yes, I believe we can. The answer to this question is not found at the Vatican, The Assemblies of God Headquarters, the Southern Baptist Convention, nor any other ecclesiastical body. The conclusive and definitive answer to this question is found in the Word of God. Paul wrote in Romans 13:14 "... clothe yourself with the presence of the Lord Jesus Christ. And don't let yourself think about ways to indulge your evil desires."

To further elaborate on a suitable wardrobe, Paul writes to the Colossian believers in the third chapter of Colossians: 12 "Put on then, as God's chosen ones, holy and beloved, compassionate hearts, kindness humility, meekness, and patience, 13 bearing with one another and, if one has a complaint against another, forgiving each other; as the Lord has forgiven you, so you also must forgive. 14 And above all these put on love, which binds everything together in perfect harmony. 15 And let the peace of Christ rule in your hearts…"

Personal experience has convinced me that we will draw more seekers to Christ by adhering to His dress code than by man's. I grew up in, and was ordained by a major Pentecostal denomination that taught me, either by creed or example, that pastors should wear suits and ties in the pulpits, and set ourselves apart by our conservative physical appearance in public. As a result of this philosophy, during much of my pastoral ministry, I was seldom seen in public without suit and tie or dress slacks, and my hair styled to perfection. In addition to that, I made sure my shoes were shined and everyone outside my home recognized me as a bona fide member of the clergy. However, my pastoral life and dress code changed the day I noticed some of my neighbors avoiding interaction with me.

It began to disturb me when I approached groups of men in our community and noticed them immediately become silent and withdrawn. In my research for *Stop Going to Church,* I was convicted by the Scriptural passages that revealed Jesus as a "friend of sinners", and a man so common in his community relationships that he was accepted by most everyone but the pious religious leaders of His day.

I'm quite sure I shall never forget the day I acted on my desire to become more approachable to the un-churched in my community. Our daughter-in-law in Little Rock, Arkansas, suggested that I schedule an appointment with her hair stylist and create a whole new contemporary look for me. In retrospect, I'm sure the experience for me AND the personnel at the flashy salon would have been less traumatic had we all known what to expect.

Georgiann and I entered the salon in Little Rock and identified ourselves to the receptionist. After a short time in the waiting area, we were introduced to my stylist. His distinctive hairstyle and soft-spoken voice were perfectly conducive to the salon décor, and he was smiling from ear to ear as he greeted me. As he welcomed us to his station, he said "My receptionist told me there's a guy out there that wants a 'redo' and he looks like a preacher! I told her, that's because he IS a preacher!"

As he completed my "redo", the stylist turned my chair toward the large mirror behind me and said, "Whaddya think?" As I looked into the mirror I couldn't believe my eyes. Gone was my smooth-looking, denominationally-sanctioned, and official pastoral coiffure I had sported for almost three decades. And in its place was a short cropped version of Einstein on steroids.

When I returned to my pulpit the following Sunday, our older saints thought I had suffered an emotional breakdown and the younger crowd greeted me with "Cool Pastor…Dude!"

A short time later, I met a clerk in one of our local retail centers who inquired of my occupation. When I informed her I was a pastor, she replied, "You don't look like a pastor!" I replied, "Good!" My incognito mission was accomplished. I had lost so much though…my long, smooth hair style, my hair dryer, my three-piece suits, my stereotypical clergy identity, and the approval of my pious colleagues. But I considered it a great exchange, for I had gained the acceptance and friendship of many of the common people and the un-churched members of our community. I learned so much through that personal transition in my lifestyle, and I came to better understand why so many of the un-churched were content to be in that category.

They had observed too many pseudo-saints don their "Sunday best" one day per week while neglecting to "put on Christ" in their daily lives. I soon came to understand why Martin Luther said "The curse of a godless man can sound more pleasant in God's ears than the Hallelujah of the pious." And I came to better understand why Ghandi professed a greater appreciation for Christ than for the professing Christians he observed.

Roger Williams had a similar attitude toward the professing Christians he knew. When Williams embraced the principles of religious liberty, the New England Puritans forced him to flee for his life. Williams found refuge among the American Indians and many were converted to Christianity. When his former brethren invited him to return, Williams made the famous reply: "I would rather live with Christian savages than with savage Christians."

I suspect the pharisaical attitude of many church members down through the ages has done more damage to the spread of the Gospel and the expansion of the Kingdom of God than the overt strategies of Satan and his hordes. Further, the tendency among us all to major on minors has limited, and continues to limit, our harvest and growth. Lisa Bevere presents an excellent example of misguided emphasis in her great book, *Lioness Arising*. She tells of posting a question on Twitter and Facebook on whether or not it was appropriate for a female minister to speak in a sleeveless top. Her question prompted an intense battle with 450 responses. Lisa writes "It seemed those who were of the opinion that sleeveless is fine, and those who felt it is not, had a holy jihad of sorts. It got out of hand, and I had to delete the strand of comments."[17]

What was most revealing and alarming was the contrast between the response to the "sleeveless" issue and a statistic Lisa had posted earlier citing the fact that 50 million women are missing from earth due to gendercide, and each year another 2 million disappear. From her 35,000 contacts on Facebook, 40 responded with a comment. I identify with Lisa's question: "Are we more comfortable with women dying than we are with them leading?" Further, are we more concerned with a leader preaching in jeans than creating an atmosphere where hurting people are healed?

Not only in my personal life, but also in our local church, I have witnessed the tremendous benefits of placing more emphasis on our spiritual wardrobe than our physical. When our leaders and our congregation fully accepted the truth that the House of God is not made of brick and mortar but flesh and blood, and that we live in the sanctuary rather than visit it, our congregation began to explode in numerical and spiritual growth. Our experience has taught us that being suited for ministry often requires us to break the curse of redundancy, but the progress we attain is worth the price we pay. There is no greater joy than to witness the healing of broken hearts, the deliverance of captives, and the rescue of those who are perishing next door and across the street.

I challenge each of you who read this to consider what is more important to you… your personal opinions and preferences, or the nature and character of Christ? Would Christ be welcomed in your place of public worship if he showed up in something less than acceptable to your dress code? In light of the fact that Jesus said when we clothed the naked, cared for the sick, and visited those in prison, we visited Him, perhaps He came to us and we turned Him away! Perhaps He was the skin-head with the tattoos and piercings; or the teenager with the ball-cap on backwards. Perhaps, He was even the black couple turned away by the deacon in Pine Bluff, Arkansas. (I was there, I witnessed it, and I still grieve!)

REACHING BRIAN WARNER

He was born January 5, 1969, and was raised in Canton, Ohio. Early in life, he was sexually abused by an older boy and was influenced by a grandfather who was hooked on hard-core pornography. As a young boy, Brian was enrolled in a private Christian school. However, he was rejected by his classmates and was treated as a misfit. Although Brian was exposed to Christians and to the Truth, obviously he was repelled, rather than attracted by what he saw and heard in the "Christian" school. One can only wonder how different Brian's life would be had someone in the "faith ghetto" cared enough to get to know Brian, had entered his world, and had allowed the light of God's love to penetrate the darkness of his life.

Unfortunately, Brian's dark world became even darker. As a result, his disdain for Christianity increased. In fact, Brian grew up to be one of the most famous blasphemers of Christ and Christians of the twentieth Century. His 1996 CD, titled, *Antichrist Superstar*, was an obvious attack on the Christian faith. The first song on the album was *"Irresponsible Hate Anthem."* In the lyrics of this song, Brian wrote, "Let's just kill everyone and let your god sort them out." On another website related to his band, web-surfers are informed, "If you want to join the online church and sell your soul to the devil, please enter your name."

You may have guessed by now, Brian Warner grew up to become Marilyn Manson (His stage name a combination of Marilyn Monroe and Charles Manson). I think we in the Church should seriously question how many Brian Warners are exposed to our ministries at this very moment. How many mentally, physically, and sexually abused (and confused) individuals has God sent to us to love, accept, and share His love, and what was our response and reaction to them?

At this critical point in history, I am convinced that, if we are to obey the Great Commission and be the Light and Salt of the world, it is imperative we set aside our preferences and opinions, and open our hearts to those seeking love and acceptance. I am also convinced and convicted that we have turned away and turned off many Brian Warners by our judgmental and legalistic attitudes toward those who didn't look, talk, and behave like us. I met one of those "turned-off" individuals some time ago while on a Sunday night patrol with another member of our local Sheriff Department.

It was Sunday, July 4, when I joined one of our deputies for a 3-11 shift. Shortly after 6 PM, we received a dispatch call to respond to a rural address where a man had allegedly made terroristic threats toward his wife and a local pastor. According to the female who called 911, her husband had phoned her during the church service she was attending and threatened to come to the church and shoot her and the pastor.

A few minutes later we arrived at the address north of Russellville, Arkansas, and spoke with the wife about the situation. She informed us that her husband was at their residence and had in his possession a large caliber pistol and a deer rifle. She then provided us with his cell phone number. My deputy partner called the husband and verified that he was at home and asked permission for us to come and visit with him. Moments later we were enroute to the residence to visit with the man.

As we approached the driveway to the residence, it was evident we were in potential serious danger. From the main road to the residence we had to drive approximately a quarter mile down a straight driveway. With no trees on either side, we had a clear view of the house, and obviously whoever was in the house had a clear view of us. Although the man had given us permission to visit with him, we didn't know if he was sitting in his rocking chair patiently waiting or had a scoped-deer rifle trained on us. However, as we approached the house, we noticed the man sitting on a bucket near a fish pond, casually drinking beer, holding a rod and reel, and waiting for us to arrive.

We got out of our cruiser, crawled through a barbed-wire fence, and began to approach the gentleman. My partner introduced himself and told him we had received a report he had made terroristic threats toward his wife and her pastor. Taking a swig of beer, he calmly, but emphatically, informed us his "bitchy" wife was lying. In an attempt to calm the man's anxiety, my deputy partner informed him we were not there to accuse him, nor to arrest him, but were there to gather information and to help him.

Then, in an attempt to assure him of our sincerity, he introduced me as the Chaplain. Oops, that was a mistake! Suddenly, the atmosphere changed. The man instantly began to curse and to inform us of his dislike for the Church, for Christians, and especially for preachers. In an angry tirade, he informed us he was raised by a mother who was a Pentecostal preacher who spent her life "cramming the Bible and her religion down his throat."

At that moment I began to immediately put the pieces of the puzzle together. The fact that this man's wife was now attending the same kind of church that he had grown to despise was simply more than he could tolerate. Now to add to his frustration, a preacher was invading his space on his own property. But before he could spew his anger toward me, I asked him if the fish were biting, and what kind of fish he had in the pond. Then I complimented him on the aerator pump he had installed in the pond. I informed him I had a pond about the same size and had never been able to solve the problem with algae and mold. For the next several minutes, he informed us of the size and brand of the pump, and explained to me how to install a pump in my pond. And as he was talking to me, under my breath I was thanking God for prompting me to change the subject and avert a dangerous confrontation. In the end, we were able to avoid an arrest and mediate the conflict between the husband and wife.

As we drove away from the residence I could not avoid my feelings of empathy and identification with the angry husband. Having grown up in a church similar to the one he described, I watched the majority of my teenaged cousins leave the church in rebellion. Although they knew they needed and wanted God in their lives, they simply could not accept the strict standards we were expected to keep. Not only were we forbidden to attend movie theaters, neither could we patronize bowling alleys, skating rinks, rodeos, or most sporting events. Although I realize that the church leaders of my childhood were sincere in their opinions and the standards they imposed, I admit that I still struggle with anger for the confusion and the carnage they created among my childhood peers. May God grant us the wisdom, patience, and understanding of His nature to love, accept, and serve ALL of those Jesus died for!

At this point, I think it is appropriate to ask, "Who are welcome in our church meetings? Are drug addicts welcomed? How about prostitutes, cross-dressers, lesbians, and homosexuals?" Some time ago, I heard a pastor of a large outreach church in England relating an interaction with one of his church elders. The elder approached the pastor before a Sunday morning service, and with an urgency in his voice said "Pastor, do you realize there is a prostitute sitting in the sanctuary this morning?" The pastor responded, "Yes, brother, and I pray that eventually every prostitute in our city attends here on Sunday mornings!" Any church leader or church member who is uncomfortable with that statement needs to hear and heed the admonition from Warren Litzman. In his book *Jesus, Lost in the Church,* he wrote: "Religion confines Christians to sectarian ghettos where their vision becomes so narrow, and their love so cold, that they can only worship with birds of the same theological feather." [18]

90

CHAPTER FIFTEEN

Moneyball

Although I'm not an avid sports fan or movie enthusiast, I was both intrigued and inspired by a movie released in 2011. Moneyball was awarded "Best Picture" by the Golden Globe Awards in 2011. The movie was based on the book, *Moneyball: The Art of Winning an Unfair Game*, by Michael Lewis. Based on a true story, Moneyball has been described as a movie for anybody who has ever dreamed of taking on the system. In the movie, Brad Pitt stars as Billy Beane, the general manager of the Oakland A's, and the guy who assembles the team. Beane had an epiphany that all of baseball's conventional wisdom is wrong. Forced to reinvent his team on a tight budget, Beane had to outsmart the richer clubs. The former jock formed an unlikely partnership with Ivy League grad, Peter Brand, and began recruiting bargain players that the scouts call flawed, but all of whom had an ability to get on base, score runs, and win games. According to Wikipedia, "It's more than baseball, it's a revolution - one that challenges old school traditions and puts Beane in the crosshairs of those who say he's tearing out the heart and soul of the game."

As Georgiann and I watched the movie in our home, it occurred to us that the story line originated a couple millenniums before the game of baseball. Actually, two thousand years before the first team was fielded, Jesus Christ challenged the traditional thinking of the religious leaders of His day and brought about radical transformation.

According to a Wikipedia synopsis of the book by Lewis, the central premise of Moneyball is that the collected wisdom of baseball insiders (including players, managers, coaches, scouts, and the front office over the past century is subjective and often flawed). Statistics such as stolen bases, runs batted in, and batting average typically used to gauge players, are relics of a 19th century view of the game and the statistics that were available at the time. The book argues that the Oakland A's' front office took advantage of more empirical gauges of player performance to field a team that could compete successfully against richer competitors in Major League Baseball.

Rigorous statistical analysis had demonstrated the on-base percentage and slugging percentage are better indicators of offensive success, and the A's became convinced that these qualities were cheaper to obtain on the open market than more historically valued qualities such as speed and contact. These observations often flew in the face of conventional baseball wisdom and the beliefs of many baseball scouts and executives.

By re-evaluating the strategies that produce wins on the field, the 2002 Athletics, with approximately $41 million in salary, were competing with larger market teams such as the New York Yankees, who spent over $125 million in payroll that same season. Because of the team's smaller revenues, Oakland was forced to find players undervalued by the market, and their system for finding value in undervalued players proved to be effective.

Lewis explored several themes in the book that I found very interesting. But the theme I found most intriguing was the battle between insiders and outsiders (established traditionalists vs. upstart proponents of sabermetrics). Sabermetrics is the specialized analysis of baseball objective, empirical evidence, specifically baseball statistics that measure in-game activity. The term is derived from the acronym SABR, which stands for the Society for American Baseball Research. It was coined by Bill James, who is one of its pioneers and is often considered its most prominent advocate and public face.

In the movie, Harvard graduate, Peter Brand, utilized sabermetrics to help Billy Beane select players with the most potential, yet overlooked and underrated by the traditionalists.

As a result of his non-traditional approach, Billy Beane was branded an idiot by the traditional coaches, managers, and players. Two thousand years ago, when Jesus Christ started His ministry here on Earth, he was constantly challenged by the insiders and traditionalists. The scribes and Pharisees followed Him, accused Him, threatened Him, and ultimately had him crucified for daring to challenge the status-quo of religion.

In the church world today, those who dare to think outside the traditional box of liturgy and methodology are branded as unspiritual rebels. Yet these so-called rebels are changing the face of the church in North America by communicating with, and reaching a cultural demographic that the traditionalists ignored, rejected, and/or ostracized long ago. And as sure as the game and the empire of baseball was transformed by the technology of sabermetrics, the methodology of church work and church growth has been transformed by young technocrats willing to endure the criticisms of the insiders. However, I can't help but wonder why these transformations must be limited to the younger generation. I simply cannot accept the idea that is it God's plan for middle aged and older church leaders to hang their harps on the willows and retire to the golf course or timeshare while there is still so many fields to harvest. If this is really God's plan, someone forgot to tell one of Judah's tribe as they fought to conquer the land of Canaan.

Recorded in the Old Testament book of Joshua are the immortal words of an eighty-five year old warrior challenging a group of younger tribesmen. Caleb said, "I was forty years old when Moses, the servant of the Lord sent me from Kadesh-Barnea to spy out the land, and I brought back word to him as it was in my heart. Nevertheless, my brethren who went up with me made the heart of the people melt with fear; bur I wholly followed the Lord.....and now behold the Lord has let me live, just as He spoke, these forty-five years....and now behold I am eighty five years old today. I am still as strong today as I was in the day that Moses sent me; as my strength was then, so is it now, for war and for going out and coming in. Now then, give me this mountain!"

I am well aware that we of the grayer generation may not be playing first base on the church softball team at this point. However, I am convinced and convicted there is still room on the Kingdom Team for those who still have the passion for a lost and dying world, and possess the wisdom that comes with decades of Bible study, prayer, and hard work.

CHAPTER SIXTEEN

A Call for Unity

In the words of that great American philosopher, Rodney King, "Can't we all just get along?" If there is one environment in the world where you'd think we could expect absolute unity and peace, it would be the Church of the Lord, Jesus Christ. However, His Church is made up of human beings who have not yet earned our halos and wings. As individuals with varying temperaments, socio-ethnic backgrounds, and varying levels of spiritual growth, we present constant challenges to each other and to the leaders who attempt to guide us toward the right path.

However, our personal weaknesses and personality differences are no excuse for displaying attitudes that are so blatantly unlike Christ that we repel the very world we are called to reach. Therefore, in the final stage of this writing I issue an appeal for more patience, understanding, respect, and unity as we all face the inevitable transitions that will prevent stagnation, redundancy, and spiritual decline.

To the charter members of the local church: I appeal to you to remember it is not your church. It matters not if your family donated the land, the pews, and the organ. Remember, it is God's Church, and we are never to claim ownership nor tenured seniority. Regardless of the role God has allowed you to function in, always recall the message from the Apostle Paul in 1 Corinthians 3:6-7, "I planted the seed, Apollos watered it, but God has been making it grow." (NIV)

To the graying or geriatric members: I appeal to you to recall your younger days when you were considered the radicals for departing from some of your traditional liturgy and ritual. I appeal to you to realize that you are living in a culture significantly different than the one you grew up in, and among a people whose modes and tools of communication probably vary greatly from those with which you are most familiar and comfortable. Therefore, you may not be comfortable when the younger crowd moves or exchanges the grand piano for the electronic keyboard. And the very thought of replacing that beautiful pipe organ or Hammond/Leslie combination may be downright repulsive to you. Then, to add insult to injury, someone may dare to remove the solid oak pulpit handcrafted by your grandfather, only to replace it with a modern acrylic version, or worse yet, an aluminum table on which your youthful blue-jean-clad pastor will place his IPAD.

I appeal to you to remember that, unfortunately, many in the culture we are called to reach have never heard of Fanny Crosby, Ira Stanphill, or George Beverly Shea. And most of them have never been exposed to the heart-warming, anointed, and inspired ministries of the Gaithers or Goodmans. Frankly, I personally miss four-part harmony, brass, wind instruments, choirs, and ensembles. However, the bottom line is that the Church leaders are not here to please me, but to please God.

And finally, I appeal to you to have patience with the fact that the younger crowd is accustomed to playing and listening to their music at higher decibels than we. And unfortunately, most of the complaints we deliver to the pastoral staff members and the Sound Engineers in the back of the room will be to no avail because, very likely, the younger crowd's hearing is already so damaged they cannot comprehend what we're complaining about, and it's quite possible they can't hear anything below 120 decibels!

Remember fellow AARPians, my hair is not gray, but white. I've been engaged in church leadership for more than four decades, and have witnessed many transitions....some good, some bad. But this I know, we dare not become so rigid and immovable that we hinder the progress of God's Church and the expansion of His Kingdom, even if it requires wearing earplugs during the praise and worship sessions.

TO THE PRE-AARP GENERATION:

I appeal to you to respect and revere those who have sacrificed physically, emotionally, and financially to pave the way for you, and to provide many of the facilities and equipment that you now utilize. If not yet, you soon will discover that the majority of the unchurched crowd you are called to reach will know little or nothing of tithing, and the primary financial support for the mission of your church will come from those who have learned the joy and reward of giving. There will be some who simply cannot, or will not, make the necessary adjustments needed to move forward, and they will leave you. When this happens, love them, pray for them, and bless them as they leave. I assure you that if you keep a Christ-like attitude, God will replace the income you're losing, and some of them will return to assist you in the harvest.

I appeal to you to remember that gray hair often grows out of the soil of wisdom and experience, and though you may possess the tools and the communication skills to identify with your contemporaries, there is still much to be gleaned from the experience and wisdom of those with more miles on their odometers. The respect and honor you extend to them, and the appeal for their assistance in your mission, will be rewarded with multi-generational teamwork. At our local church, our leaders have deliberately targeted young unchurched individuals and families in our area. As a result, this group comprises the majority of our members. However, some of our most dedicated workers are in their sixties, seventies, and eighties. These faithful veterans have come to understand that the value of the harvest is much greater than their personal preferences, opinions, and traditions.

ANY REGRETS?

Having gone through numerous transitions in forty-three years of full-time ministry, do I have any regrets? Sure, don't we all? I regret having to leave close friends behind in order to move on with God's call on my life. I regret that many of those I love have misunderstood my motives and questioned my methods.

I regret feeling compelled to forsake my denominational heritage and affiliation for a season to preserve my marriage, my family, and the young converts who had come to know the practical love of Jesus.

However, I am so grateful that God is merciful and gracious, that *goodness and mercy* still follow me to clean up my messes. I am grateful that God has given a special lady named Georgiann, the courage and grace to stand by my side for more than four decades, in good and bad times, for better and for worse. I am grateful that God spared our three children the bitterness and cynicism that could have trapped and destroyed them during our battles with religion and redundancy.

Is progress worth the price? In light of eternal souls and their destiny, yes! I recently stepped into a local floral shop to purchase a bouquet for Georgiann. The proprietor, whom I hadn't seen in several years, recognized me and said, "I need to share something with you. I know the price you and your family have paid in this city to follow your calling, and I want to personally thank you for not giving up. For because you were willing to stand and fight for what you believe, there is another powerful church in this city. Because you did not run, there is a church called *The Journey*, reaching a group of people that no one else was reaching." I so appreciated the compliment and I honestly needed the encouragement. But that's not the compliment I'm really longing for. I am longing for the day when I can hear my heavenly Father say, "Well done, good and faithful servant!" Only then will I truly know the reward is worth every tear, every heartache, every separation, every mis-understanding, and every painful transition in the battle against dead traditions, Pharisaism, and redundancy. And the joy of seeing lives transformed here and now will be just a preview of the ecstasy we will experience together in the eternal realm.

CHAPTER SEVENTEEN

Valuable Lessons Learned

In four decades of transition I have learned thirteen very important lessons. They are as follows.

1. The church is not a building but a people, therefore,

2. We do not GO to church, we ARE the Church.

3. The Sanctuary is not in a building but in our hearts.

4. We are called to be the light of the world, not the light of the Church.

5. Most churches are strong on meetings but weak on services.

6. Nowhere in Scriptures are we commanded to "Go to church", but are commanded to "Go to the world."

7. Anointed preaching can not be measured with a decibel meter. This was a difficult lesson for someone brought up in a Pentecostal denomination in an era and atmosphere without public address systems. The speakers of that era had to yell for their messages to be heard. Somewhere along the way, anointing was equated with volume. Consequently, the louder and more rapidly a speaker could preach, the greater his anointing!

I learned this painful lesson in the early days of my ministry when I overheard a child say "Mommy, why is he yelling at us?"

The lesson was further driven home to me when Dr. Wayne Kraiss from Vanguard University was our pulpit guest in the early Seventies. In his calm, conversational style, he delivered one of the most powerfully-anointed messages I had ever heard.

Take home point: People want to be talked to, not preached at, screamed or yelled at.

8. We often are guilty of answering questions no one is asking. (Another series on *"The Five Hebrew Words for Worship"* might be inspiring, but may not address the challenges your congregants are facing.)

9. We often speak a language that is foreign to the un-churched. Our not-yet-converted friends and guests probably won't understand our pontificating on the virtues of being "washed in the blood", being "slain", or "baptized with the Holy Ghost."

10. Hymns are not limited to Luther, Wesley, or our denominational hymnals.

11. Altars are not limited to furniture in the front of our meeting rooms, but should be located in the center of our hearts.

12. We cannot honestly say we want the un-churched to join us while expecting them to "look, sound, and behave" churchy. If you really desire to be an outreach church, become accustomed to cigarette butts near your entrance, and don't be too shocked when someone publicly compliments you with "Hell of a sermon, Reverend!", or a female convert comes out of the baptismal water, embraces you, and plants a kiss squarely on your mouth. (Yes, it happened to me!) Remember the words of Luther: "The curse of a godless man can sound more pleasant in God's ears than the Hallelujah of the pious." (Thank you, Marty!)

13. There really are Christians outside my denomination who will make it to heaven, albeit probably on the second load! (Oh, lighten up, Deacon Jones, I was joking!)

CHAPTER EIGHTEEN

Transitional Messages

Many of today's cutting-edge churches are mistakenly viewed as *overnight successes* or *watered-down* versions of the true Church. Unfortunately, in most cases these judgments are made by jealous religious leaders or observers simply ignorant of the facts.

The transition and growth of our local church in Arkansas took years of pain, patience, and persistence by those who were leading and those willing to be led. You have read the story of our journey in previous chapters. Along the way, we have shared with you the pain of our progress. You may have laughed or cried with us, or you may be critical of our methods and our decisions. We humbly admit we have made many mistakes and would do things differently if we could retrace our steps. However, in God's grace and mercy, though we have not arrived, we have survived and are continuing to seek God's wisdom in reaching and discipling the world around us.

TRANSITION TAKES TIME AND PATIENCE

For those of you who feel the need to transition to an Outreach Church, please understand that each situation and each demographic requires different strategies. No established, introverted church will transition quickly, so be prepared to turn the ship slowly, methodically, and very prayerfully, lest you end up with a major shipwreck. We do not suggest that you try to duplicate our methods. However, it may be helpful for us to share some of the lessons and messages delivered in our *Huddle* sessions over a period of three years in the transition period from The Life Center to The Journey. (*Huddles* were weekly sessions conducted for everyone willing to come and hear the mission and vision of the church.) Feel free to use any of these messages in any way that will assist you in your arena and stage of transition. (No need to credit us. Just tell your people you read it in MY book! :) Note that some of the earlier messages will refer to Life Center and others will refer to The Journey as the church transitioned. I will insert comments along the way to clarify some of the transitional steps.

REDUNDANT RELIGION OR RELEVANT GOD

HUDDLE 01/05/02. In this session, Steve shared the following:

"Let us look back at the past year and remember the good, the bad, and the downright ugly. The past year was a year of transition. We were a transitioning church. Through the transition, we had to face the hard questions and not just face them, but answer them: What is the purpose of the Church? What has God called Life Center to be? How have we done the past few years? What is wrong with this picture? How can we better be and do what God has called us to be and do? Is it possible for a church in Russellville, Arkansas to reach the un-churched and de-churched?

As we began to not only ask the questions, but seek the answers and make the hard decisions to move us to God's original design, we began to see changes. Something changed on the inside of me. I began to change as a leader. I began to be gripped by God's heart for the world and a vision that his Church could, and should be, the vehicle to make a difference. I was gripped once again by the reality that God really could do something incredible, build a church with a tithe of the city of Russellville in it, (A vision God gave my Dad in 1990) and that Life Center should be that place. As we began last year with the transition of the Pastoral role here at Life Center, the end result in mind was the fulfillment of that vision.

It's been said that if you always do what you've always done, you'll get what you've always gotten. In other words, what you have is a result of what you've done. If I don't like the outcome of my use of time, I should change my use of time. If my marriage is not like I think it could be, I need to make some changes in how I treat my relationship with my spouse.

If my business is not where I want it to be, perhaps I need to make some business changes. Change hurts. I have to give up something to make the reality of a better marriage happen. It might be golf, the newspaper, my Playstation 2, or that second job, but if I want the results of a better marriage, I will go through the pain. The Church is no different. If we were to become the Church that God had in mind when he spoke to our founding Pastor in 1990, then we had to change. We did!

- We decided to be fishers of men and were forced to identify the fish in our city.

- We developed a new Mission Statement: Genuine Faith, Authentic people, Relevant God.

We also determined to be genuine...real.

- Real Faith: we own it and we maintain it.

- Real People: What you see is what you get. This changed the way we dressed, the way we presented ourselves and therefore, the image of our church.

- Real God, Relevant: Good for the moment.

- We changed the way we did church: Our music, our messages, the length of our messages, our methods and our topics.

- We changed the way we do evangelism: We took His love to the streets with: Hot chocolate, trash collection, free cokes, free water, free gasoline, car washes, and window washing.

- We converted to topical messages. Something to leave with and act upon to make life different today. Interactive messages that are experiential, image based, and connecting.

As we stand at the open door leading us into another year, we are no longer a transitioning church. We have been born again. We have gone through the labor, the struggles, the pain, the separation, the anxiety, and the financial stresses of bringing new life into the world. But I have an announcement to make: THE BABY HAS ARRIVED AND IT IS DOING FINE!

The objective for us in the next 12 months is to stay the course. We must not grow weary in doing good, for we will reap a harvest if we faint not. We must persevere in the race. The truth of the matter is that the year of transition, loss, and pruning is over, and after a good pruning always comes a record harvest. The heart of Life Center is to be the Church; to love God and to love others into a relationship with God. The heart is right and the methods and principles are working. We have read the Bible, we have read the culture, and we have brought the Word to the culture at hand as the Apostle Paul and Jesus Himself taught us through example. And the kingdom of God is growing in the hearts of men.

Is there still work to do? Yes. Are there still areas where we are somewhat weak? Yes. Are there areas that need our attention? Yes. We are aware of those and are endeavoring to shore up all loose ends, and recruit and train people for areas of ministry."

A RELEVANT GOD

We advise pastors who desire to become Outreach-focused, to set aside time to study the methods of church leaders who are effective at reaching the un-churched world around them. We have found it very valuable to take our staff, our board members (and spouses, if possible) to conventions and to churches where the vision of outreach is taught and modeled. Then once you have caught the vision and the heart of God for your church, begin sharing it weekly with everyone who will listen! During our transitional phase, Steve took several staff members to Texas to visit and examine a church successfully connecting with thousands of un-churched individuals in the Dallas/Fort Worth area.

The following are some excerpts from Steve's message via video from Texas on a *Relevant God*:

"Hi, Welcome to SNL, Saturday Night Life at Life Center. For those of you who don't know, I am Steve Pyle, the lead Pastor around here. You might be wondering why I am talking to you via video. Well, the staff and I are in Dallas, Texas, at Fellowship Church.com for the Creative Church Conference. We are studying hard what some of the most effective churches in America are doing to become and stay relevant to a constantly changing culture. These churches are setting the standard when it comes to communicating the awesome message of Christ to people who have rejected the church's methods of communicating it for the past 20 years. I hope to be sharing some of what we're learning with you in the weeks to come. Perhaps even WE can become creative communicators.

For the past few weeks, we have really been getting into the vision that God has for us and our vision for what we want to become individually and as a group. We have discussed being people of Genuine Faith, a people who really live the way we say we believe. Last week we discussed being Authentic People, a *What you see is what you get people;* a people who know that we've got problems; we know that we're not perfect but rely on what Jesus did for us to make us right. Because we understand how messed up we are, we can accept everyone right where they are. If God can accept us, then we can accept others. We don't pretend to be anything more than what we are: broken people being put back together by a loving God.

This evening/morning, whenever you are experiencing this, I want to pose some questions and hopefully provoke your thinking along the lines of a Relevant God. You see, I believe that God lives in the today In our town. He speaks our language, he knows our likes, dislikes, our needs and wants, our problems, our sin, and He loves us very much, and wants to have a relationship with each of us. The word relevant means that it's good for the moment, meets the need, and it is related to the matter at hand. I shared in huddle last week that 42% of those who do not attend church feel that the church is irrelevant to their lives. I think we are misrepresenting the Relevant God. I think we can do better, don't you?

Let's begin by laying a biblical foundation for our discussion today.

1 Corinthians 9:19-23: "Though I am free and belong to no man, I make myself a slave to everyone, to win as many as possible. To the Jews I became like a Jew, to win the Jews. To those under the law I became like one under the law (though I myself am not under the law), so as to win those under the law. To those not having the law I became like one not having the law (though I am not free from God's law but am under Christ's law), so as to win those not having the law. To the weak I became weak, to win the weak. I have become all things to all men so that by all possible means I might save some. I do all this for the sake of the gospel that I may share in its blessings." (NIV)

As Steve showed a video clip of the movie *Sister Act,* we saw that the church was empty and unprofessional, with time-warped, irrelevant presentations, and an uninviting atmosphere with boring messages.

Steve challenged the congregation with the following review:

"What could this church do to become effective again at reaching its community?"

In the second video clip we saw the empty church building begin to fill up as the church began to move in the direction of the people. Something had changed in the way they did church that caused people to come through the doors without the church changing any of its core beliefs or teaching.

Can the church remain relevant without change or misunderstanding?

In the third video clip, there was an argument over musical style, servant evangelism, and connecting with the people. Something happened that caused life to come back into this church. The people began to do something that made the change in their city. Can you remember and recount what that was?

It's not just what we do in our corporate gathering that makes the difference, although that plays a big role. It's what each

108

member does in their individual lives everyday that makes the difference in the relevance of the Church to the world.

It's being people of genuine faith, who live out what we say we believe. Being authentic, not pretending to be perfect, but acknowledging we don't have all the answers, leaning on and believing in Jesus to make up for our inadequacies. We are becoming relevant, individually and corporately, so that God who is always relevant can be revealed to the world again through His Church.

In closing, I think if Jesus were here with us today, He would say something like, 'I was driving past McDonald's the other day and saw that playground and it made me think,' or 'I see your reading *How to be Happy Though Married*...I'd like to talk to you about that,' or 'I noticed while watching 20/20 last night that lots of people are struggling with fear.' You see, Jesus was concerned with where people were, with what they were dealing with, and He met them there, ministered to them there, and then introduced them to His father. He informed His followers that if they had seen Him, they had seen the Father. And then He left and told us to be His representation.

Can we say 'If you've seen me/us, you've seen the father?' Are we revealing a relevant God? If not, shouldn't we change in order to be what God wants us to be....a true reflection of him? Let's pray."

NOBLE EFFORTS VS COMMITMENT TO CHRIST

Several months before I transitioned from senior-pastor I, Larry, used a video clip from *Saving Private Ryan,* during a Sunday morning meeting, to illustrate sacrificial love for others. It was a "moving" experience to say the least. So moving, in fact, that it moved one of our key families right out the door. Unfortunately, they were offended by my exposing their children to an "R" rated movie, albeit a 5 minute clip. And unfortunately for us, we lost both our Royal Rangers Leader and our Missionettte Leader. Fortunately for Steve, I had already offended and shifted many of those who loved us, but couldn't ride with us.

From the time Steve received the baton from me in 2002, he met with a group of potential leaders each Sunday night for three years. In these sessions, Steve constantly repeated the mission and vision statement of the church.

In one of the Sunday evening Huddles, Steve challenged the congregation with the following message that every transitional leader needs to hear and heed:

Dedication to a dream:

"Greetings to all of you gathered here this evening. There is a good chance that right now at this moment I am reclining on the beach reading a good book as the wind blows through my hair. But I felt so strongly about being present to communicate my thoughts with you that I took time last week to record this message for you. There is nothing in this entire world that could be more important than what we will be sharing with you this evening.

Remember, seeker-sensitive churches are meaningless without seeker sensitive Christians. My question is this, are you in agreement with me to become people who give themselves away? People who give themselves 100% to God, to each other, and to the world? If so, then buckle your seat belt because we're about to blow!

Church, there are multiple projects and ministries we can give our lives to: We can volunteer time for the Boys and Girls Clubs, PTA, coaching little league, or running for public office; We can dedicate time and energy to the Area Agency for the Aged, Meals on Wheels, or one of many other civic-serving organizations. All of these are organizations and are worthy of our time and monetary contribution. However, all of these agencies and organizations combined will never get to the core of the problems facing those around us.

The bottom line is this: None of these organizations or causes can change a human heart. They can't heal a wounded soul. They can't turn hatred into love. They can't bring about repentance, forgiveness, reconciliation, or peace. Only the love of Jesus can!

The truth is that the Church is the only hope for the world to see and experience that love.

God's intention is for a team of people working as a body to fulfill his purpose in the earth. Things that begin small can grow huge because they begin with unparalleled dedication by the few that becomes the *standard* for the many."

CHAPTER NINETEEN

Transition Requires Teamwork

STEVE:

PARTICIPATION IN THE DREAM

Margaret Mead once said, "Never believe that a few caring people can't change the world. For indeed, that's all who ever have."

Mrs. Mead's statement presents a strong contrast with a scene that occurred on a New York street nearly two decades ago. Kitty Genovese was slowly and brutally stabbed to death. At least thirty-eight of her neighbors witnessed the attack and heard her screams. In the course of the 90-minute episode, her attacker was actually frightened away, then returned to finish her off. Yet not once during that period did any neighbor assist her, or even telephone the police. The implications of this tragic event shocked America, and it stimulated two young psychologists, Darly and Latane, to study the conditions under which people are, or are not willing to help others in an emergency. In essence, they concluded that responsibility becomes diffused. The more people present in an emergency situation, the less likely it is that any one of them will offer help. This is popularly called the "Bystander Effect." (In the actual experiment, when one bystander was present, 85 percent offered help. When two were present, 62 percent offered help. When five were present, then it decreased to 31 percent.)

"The salvation of mankind lies only in making everything the concern of all." Alexander Solzhenitsyn

We have an opportunity to create something incredible. We've been given a mandate from God and I believe the only thing keeping us from possessing the church that God envisioned in the birth of Life Center in 1990 is the question: Are willing vessels made available for God to use to create it?

A pastor once made an investment in a large piece of ranch real estate which he hoped to enjoy during his years of retirement. While he was still an active pastor, he would take one day off each week to go out to his land and work. But what a job! What he had bought, he soon realized, was several acres of weeds, gopher holes, and rundown buildings. It was anything but attractive, but the pastor knew it had potential and he stuck with it.

Every week he'd go to his ranch, crank up his small tractor, and plow through the weeds with a vengeance. Then he'd spend time doing repairs on the buildings. He'd mix cement, cut lumber, replace broken windows, and work on the plumbing. It was hard work, but after several months the place began to take shape. And every time the pastor put his hand to some task, he would swell with pride. He knew his labor was finally paying off.

When the project was completed, the pastor received a neighborly visit from a farmer who lived a few miles down the road. Farmer Brown took a long look at the preacher and cast a longer eye over the revitalized property. Then he nodded his approval and said, "Well preacher, it looks like you and God really did some work here." The pastor, wiping the sweat from his face, answered, "It's interesting you should say that, Mr. Brown. But I've got to tell you, you should have seen this place when God had it all to Himself!"

The only way things become as God envisions them is for people to get involved in the process! You know, it's frustrating at times when you are leading a Non-Profit organization because you know that what you do is of utmost importance. However, Non-Profits only function with the blood, sweat, and tears of true believers who own the goals of the organization.

Have you ever noticed that those who stand on the sidelines always have an opinion of how those in the game should be doing something different? According to the much-quoted Toomey's Rule: "It is easy to make decisions on matters for which you have no responsibility."

John Jay Chapman said, "You can get assent to almost any proposition so long as you are not going to do anything about it."

It is interesting that Nehemiah never prayed for God to rebuild the wall. What he prayed for was an opportunity to rebuild it himself. That is the difference between a dreamer and a visionary. Dreamers dream about things being different. Visionaries envision themselves making things different.

Dreamers think about how nice it would be for things to be done, while visionaries look for an opportunity to do something. I have invited each of you here tonight because I believe that you are called of God to be a visionary in this house...to be a driving force, engaged in the accomplishing of the vision of God in the River Valley through the Journey.

Possibly you say, "Who Me?" Everybody can be great, because anybody can serve. You don't have to have a college degree to serve. You don't have to make your subject and verb agree to serve. Martin Luther King, Jr. said, "You only need a heart full of grace...a soul generated by love."

In a non-profit organization, the success of the organization lies at the feet of each participant. If we fail to become what God has envisioned for the Journey, the words of Barry Beck of the New York Rangers ring true in our case, "We have only one person to blame, and that's each other."

You are here tonight because I believe that it is no accident that you are a participant of the Journey. I believe that God has placed you here to be a vital part in the leadership. I believe that we will only become what God has ordained as you and I both put our heads in the yoke and begin to pull. Will you join me in this quest?

Will you help me share the journey with the River Valley? Together we will rise or fall. I prefer to Rise."

SECURITY, IS A POOR SUBSTITUTE FOR DESTINY

STEVE CONTINUES: "In any organization, when security becomes the substitute for destiny, the organization is headed for redundancy. However, security is a poor substitute for destiny!

We all must be committed to moving forward to the next level. Until one is committed, there is hesitancy, the chance to draw back, always producing ineffectiveness. With that in mind, consider the following quotes:

"Concerning all acts of initiative (and creation) there is one elementary truth, the ignorance of which kills countless ideas and splendid plans: that the moment one definitely commits oneself, then providence moves too." (Johann Wolfgang von Goethe, 1749-1832)

"The stationary condition is the beginning of the end."
Henri Amiel

When we settle for normal, when we stop at good enough, when we cease from looking for more, we have begun our own death march. Some has said, "You become an old dog, when you stop learning new tricks." Are we content to stay as we have been, or to remain as we are? Do we believe that God still has something better in our future than in our past? Then why is it so hard for us to let go, to latch onto greatness?

"Is life so dear, or peace so sweet, as to be purchased at the price of chains or slavery? Forbid it, Almighty God! I know not what course others may take but as for me; give me liberty or give me death!"
Patrick Henry

"Give me God's dream or give me death! Nothing else will satisfy. We cannot become what we need to be, remaining what we are."
Max Depree

PURPOSE DRIVEN PROGRAM DEVELOPMENT

It has been said that a program is the sum total of a church's actions employed to achieve its mission. Programs are developed to promote/accomplish the mission. A problem arises when mission becomes promotion of the program. Programs which do not accomplish the mission must be renovated or removed.

A problem develops when people identify mission as the program without asking if the program is accomplishing a mission. We may begin developing our program only after we have determined our mission. Without each of us understanding what our mission is, we may not all understand the reasoning behind the program. Once we clearly understand our mission, developing a program to accomplish it becomes easier by asking two questions:

1. Does this help uncommitted people (un-churched, de-churched, nominal Christians) become followers of Christ?

2. Does this help followers of Christ become better followers of Christ?

Does our program help people, whatever their background, become better people (disciples, more like Christ) and in doing so please, honor, obey and glorify God? Once again, the mission is not either/or but both/and, therefore our program must accomplish both objectives.

Unfortunately, churches can grow from a membership-transfer relatively easily because most churches program for church people. But what about the ½ of the U.S. adult population who are un-churched? Church leaders would never be so brash and insensitive and truly un-Christ-like to say that they don't want to win others to Christ, but how many ever truly do what is necessary to do that? And, why is this? Because it is easy for us to fall into a trap of communicating to one group of people. If the pastor decides that the mission dictates changing the way he communicates, he runs the risk of losing the very people who enjoy the way he has communicated in the past.

"That's the risk you take if you change: that people you've been involved with won't like the new you. But other people who do will come along." Lisa Alther

"The mission is always worth whatever programmatic change is necessary to see it accomplished. If churches and pastors don't change, can the church still accomplish its mission?" Evangelism that Works, Barna

"What we need is not better interpretation, but better application." Rick Warren

"Allow people the time to go through the process." Engle Scale/Gray Matrix

Overall 85% of un-churched Americans were once churched. Every American has access to the Gospel. However, we cannot conclude that every American has heard or understood the gospel. Until we communicate so that all understand, we haven't communicated, we've only made noise. We must create a comfortable environment where all can hear a practical message from the scriptures. I want everyone who comes through our doors to leave thinking "I didn't know that was there. That was actually understandable and helpful."

REMEMBER. THE SERMON BEGINS IN THE PARKING LOT!

What will people experience when they arrive at our building? The Love of God! Remember, the sermon begins in the parking lot. The greeters at the doors help present the sermon; the workers in the nurseries; the teachers in the classes; those enjoying fellowship in the Living Room; the workers at the hospitality table, and the corporate service itself are all presenters of the message for the day. God loves individuals. Christ died for them. He is the way to eternal life and we all are presenters of His message.

"A healthy church should have a mixture of 3 groups of people 1.) Not Yet Saved 2.) Recently Saved 3.) Mature Believers attending." Ed Young

If everyone is mature: We are failing at the Great Commission. If everyone is a baby: We are failing at discipleship. If we are to be a healthy church, we must maintain and grow all three groups of people. In order to maintain and grow each group of people we must identify and address the needs of each group of people.

There must be grace in the growing. All too often, we want to clean the fish before we catch them. However, God does the cleaning, not the church. It's vital that we understand the difference between law and liberty.

What are the needs of the Not-Yet Saved?

1. Acceptance: Process of Decision
2. Word: Discipleship
3. Worship: Fellowship with God
4. Fellowship: Accountability

What are the needs of the Recently Saved?

1. Acceptance: Process of sanctification
2. Word: Discipleship
3. Worship
4. Fellowship and Accountability

What are the needs of the Mature Believer?

1. Word: Corporate Gathering, Cell, Discipleship
2. Worship: Corporate Gathering; encourage personal time with God
3. Fellowship: Corporate Gathering, Cell, Accountability
4. Outlet: Opportunity to offer service.

Last week we dealt with the question or at least posed the question: "To what degree does reaching new people and leading them to faith in Jesus shape the culture of our church?"

A definition of Culture would be this: The people with whom you live, the values of the people with whom you live, the language of the people with whom you live, the music of the people with

118

whom you live, and the art of the people with whom you live shapes your culture. In today's culture rule #1 is: the medium is the message.

DEFINING OUR IDENTITY

To define our church's identity we must clearly understand our mission. This creates a foundation which is something solid to stand for and boundaries that we may stay within when deciding what to do and what not to do. This reveals our heart's passion and prioritizes our ministry offerings. It directs our resources and focuses our goals. Our mission statement becomes this: We exist to experience genuine faith, become authentic people, and reveal a relevant God to a watching world.

In addition to defining the identity of our local church, it is critical to understand the culture around us. In order to do that, we need to study the geographics, the demographics, and the psychographics of the community around us.

WHAT ARE THE GEOGRAPHICS?

We need to clearly understand those who make up our culture. Who is our community? What are the geographics (the physical proximity of individual households in the community to the church and to each other measured in miles or time)? It is said that 80% of a congregation lives within five miles of the church location.

WHAT ARE THE PSYCHOGRAPHICS?

Psychographics refer to the values, attitudes, likes, dislikes, needs, and shared cultural experiences of the members of the community. This includes: Concern for children, valuing their time, and caring about their music. Where are they on the spiritual seeking scale? (Engle scale)

We must determine whether or not these individuals are hostile, neutral, seeking, inactive, or active believers? Without knowing or realizing it, most churches sincerely desire to reach the neutrals, seeking, and inactive believers with "active believer" messages.

WHAT ARE THE DEMOGRAPHICS?

Demographics determine the characteristics of groups of people in the community, classified by sex, age, race, income, etc. Knowing the demographics helps us prioritize our ministries.

1. If 80% of those who are most likely to be reached by our church don't have children, do we need to spend lots of money and energy on children's programs? No. However, if 80% of those do have children, that changes our focus considerably doesn't it?

2. If 50% of those are single parents, perhaps then a ministry for single parents or a childcare ministry during the summer might become a top priority for us in reaching our community. Do you see how clearly understanding who it is we are called to reach can determine our identity?

In his excellent book *Seeing Beyond Church Walls*, Steve Sjogren writes: "Those countless others are secretly waiting for an angel with an epidermis to show up. They're waiting for someone who will laugh, hoist a couch, give them places to sleep when their spouses kick them out, find a dentist, listen to their questions, buffet their anger, cry with them in emergency rooms, go to the movies with them, or just commune over cold hot-dogs when the power shuts down. In this post-Christian dispersion, our front doors are more likely to be carved out of cluttered living rooms, grocery lines, prison lobbies, and bar stools than three thousand dollars worth of steel and glass. These are great acts. People who do these things understand the main thing. It is in this area that we as leaders of a movement must be willing to take risks. The Bible tells us that it's better to leave the harvest in the field than to harvest with no place to put it. The harvest is truly plentiful and the laborers are few, but growing."

"Peter Wagner has said if we do not get the people in our churches connected within the first two years, we will lose them out the back door. His statement proved to be true in my own pastoral ministry at that time. A few years later, I found the time window to be shortened to one year, then six months, then three months. Now it's more like two or three weeks."[19]

It's time to become like Christ, true Christians. It's time to make the main thing, the main thing and keep it the main thing. It's time to invest our lives in relationships with others to lead them into a genuine love relationship with Father God. I am asking you to begin to do this.

HUDDLE MESSAGE: 10/06/02

Steve's message to the Journey:

In the early seventies, there was a Bible College professor named Dr. Gilbert Bilezekian who taught New Testament studies. Bill Hybels, Sr. Pastor of Willow Creek Community Church, was one of his students.

Bill was expecting a snore-class under his professor. However, the professor rocked his world with this:

"Students, there was once a community of believers who were so totally devoted to God that their life together was charged with the Spirit's power. In that band of Christ-followers, believers loved each other with a radical kind of love. They took off their masks and shared their lives with one another. They laughed, and cried, and prayed, and served together in authentic Christian fellowship. Those who had more shared freely with those who had less until socioeconomic barriers melted away. People related together in ways that bridged gender and racial chasms, and celebrated cultural differences. Acts 2 tells us that this community of believers, this church, offered unbelievers a vision of life that was so beautiful it took their breath away. It was so bold, so creative, so dynamic that they couldn't resist it. Verse 47 tells us that "the Lord added to their number daily those who were being saved."[20]

If the students were asleep up to that point, they woke up when he began to tell that story. Bill said, "That day, I didn't just see the vision, I was seized by it."

As I heard that, my response is the same as that described by Bill. Where had that beauty gone? Why was that power not evident in the contemporary church? Would the Christian community ever see that potential realized again? With all my heart, I want our local church to regain and reveal the power and the passion of Christ to the world around us.

One of my heroes in the faith is Steve Sjogren, the guru of servant evangelism. He said this: "While we all know the truth of the verse, *I will build my church and the gates of Hades will not overcome it,* the real question today is, will the church survive another generation of its own inwardly-focused gaze?"

Folks, if the vision of the Church expressed by the good Bible College professor raised your blood pressure or caused your heart to speed up, then you are in the right place because that is what we are!

In the introduction to his book, *Courageous Leadership,* Bill Hybels tells about being at Ground Zero ten days after September 11th. Workers were still digging feverishly to find survivors and the bodies of victims. Listen to his words on pages 14 and 15:

"No matter how incomprehensible was the scene surrounding me, the enormity of the evil behind it could not be denied. But strangely, while the ashes smoldered around me and grief overwhelmed me, even then, a profound hope rose in my heart. Slicing through the anguished 'no ways' reverberating in my mind were the words I had repeated ten thousand times before, but now they cut with the flash of urgency. *The local church is the hope of the world.* I could see it so clearly."[21]

THE LOCAL CHURCH IS THE HOPE OF THE WORLD!

Let's be that church. Steve Sjogren writes in his book *Seeing Beyond Church Walls*: "In my first book, I said that we have to face the fact that having seeker-sensitive services counts for little if we don't have seeker– sensitive Christians. In other words, if our Christians don't love (and like) non-Christians, then all our talk about change and renewal won't mean beans. But if our Christians DO love and like non-Christians, then watch out! Jesus summarized his mission with clarity. Roughly paraphrased, the mission is: *Love God. Love people.* The rest are details."[22]

The question we must face today as a local church is: "Are we going to be people of genuine faith?" Do we really love and value others? Do we really believe that giving a glass of water in God's name is the same as giving it to God himself? Do we really believe that ministering to another human being is the same as ministering unto God? If we do my friends, then the proof will be in the pudding. We will not just wrangle for religion. We may write for it, fight for it and die for it; but we will live for it?

"Yes, we had a mission statement; what we lacked was a mission."— Richard L. Dunagin

It is one thing to have a mission statement but it's another thing all together to, as an individual, have a mission.

HUDDLE MESSAGE: 11/10/02

A couple of weeks ago I talked to you about the concept of creating and cultivating ethos as being the primary goal of leadership. Ethos is a spontaneous recurring pattern, which is a natural response, not legislated. It is something everyone in your community does without having to be told.

The church that I grew up in, and probably many you as well, was a community of people who lived by certain rules. We were identified by what we did not do, rather than what we did. If someone asked about my church I would tell them about our music. Then I'd tell them what made us different by giving them a list of what we did not do that others did. You know the list...we don't lie, cheat, gamble, cuss, drink alcohol, smoke, dip or chew tobacco, watch R-rated movies, dress immodestly, tell dirty jokes, laugh at dirty jokes, think of dirty anything, lust or look at pornography; nor do we believe in abortion, listen to "secular music", watch television....and the list goes on and on. I can't blame them for the response I got most of the time...an uninterested "OH!"

Remember when I told you that it was more important to change what people care about than to change what people believe? We can believe a lot of things and not care about any of them. However, ethos are those things that we do, not because were supposed to, but because that is who we are. God had in mind a Church that really did love Him with all their heart, soul, mind and strength. He really was desirous of a Church that, because of their relationship with Him, had His heart and His character and really could love their neighbor as themselves. It becomes much more about a distinguishable lifestyle of those who are followers of Christ.

We live a certain way because with Christ in us, we are totally different. Imagine with me, if you can, a different scenario. You and I have been completely changed by a relationship with Jesus Christ. We love him with all our heart, soul, mind and strength and that relationship has completely changed the way we relate to others.

We have embraced the concept that "I am not" and are allowing "I am" to live through us. We have resolved to do two things well....Love God and Love people. Where the world around us is unkind, we excel in kindness. Where the world around us is uncaring, we care. Where the world around us is selfish, we are selfless. Where the world around us is calloused, we love. Where the world around is isolating, we are accepting of all. Think about a group of people who display out-of-control levels of kindness, unselfishness, generosity, acceptance, and compassion. What a vision for the Church!

Wouldn't it be incredible if the Church became so spontaneous and outward that observers would comment, "Look, another outburst of love and good deeds." Maybe you think it is impossible. I say it's totally possible!

That is what God had in mind from the beginning. Jesus came and showed us how to live a life of relationship with the

Father, which leads to a self-sacrificing love for others. In fact, He modeled this so perfectly in Matthew 14. Jesus hears of his cousin John being beheaded and just tries to get away to be alone. When He reaches the shore, a crowd of people who have great physical needs meets him. Jesus feels compassion on them and heals their sickness and disease. In His time of need, He is thinking of others. Now that is different. He didn't do that because He was supposed to, but because that is who He was.

The people knew that if they had a need, they could come to Jesus. Wouldn't it be great if the same could be said about his representatives? Leadership is about creating ethos. We are interested in becoming people who love God so intensely that we possess His heart and His character, out of which we love the world into a relationship with Him.

We are creating and cultivating an ethos here at Life Center. We want to keep the main thing, the main thing: Personal relationship with Christ, which leads to living the Christ life for the benefit of others. We have tried, with little sustained fruit, to focus on methods and the "latest thing" going on in the church around the world. What we have lacked is a people who have embraced not only the message of Christ, but the Christ-life. This is the ethos of Life Center.

No longer will we be defined by what we don't do because of what we believe, but known by what we do because of who we are. We will be known for what we do rather than what we say, what we believe, our current programs or the buildings we meet in.

CHAPTER TWENTY

The Relational Pain of Progress

Making the transition from a church for Christians to a church for everyone is not an easy move for a traditional congregation. For starters, it will challenge your theology, your opinions and preferences, and possibly the sterility of your comfort zone. Although our church was launched with the expressed idea of reaching the unreached, touching the untouched, and loving the unloved, we really had no understanding of what that would cost us.

In spite of our noble ideas of reaching people other churches were ignoring, most of us were born and raised in churches that existed for Christians. And the truth is, we had become so sterilized that, in spite of our annual missions conventions and monthly missions offerings, we really had no concept of what it meant to actually open our hearts and our doors to the un-churched. For most of us, a musical video of *People need the Lord* could bring us to tears. However, the thought of those addicts, criminals and "un-churchy" folks actually sharing our pews, dining halls, and youth centers was too much for some among us.

Honestly, I thought I had effectively communicated our vision for Life Center and our mission to reach those others were ignoring. After all, my first book on the purpose and mission of the Ecclesia was born out of a fourteen month series of messages intended to move our salt out of the shaker. However, when we actually took Him to the streets, many of the street folks followed us

126

home. At first we were excited and so proud that we displayed them like trophies, having them share their public testimonies for all to hear. But unfortunately, many of them didn't Christianize as quickly as we envisioned; In fact, they soiled our couches, stained our carpets, and even cussed in front of our kids.

I suppose I should not have been so shocked when one of our elders informed me that some of our folks disapproved of their kids having to associate with "unsaved" teenagers at our church meetings. After all, the fact that they spent five days per week with the pot-smoking, vulgar little rebels was proof enough they needed a sanctuary where they could escape on Wednesdays and Sundays.

Let me pause here long enough to climb up on my soap box and vent. I feel that I wasted too many years of my life and ministry tolerating (and probably practicing) the hypocrisy, legalism, and judgmentalism that grows like weeds in the soil of the religious ghettos. And frankly, at this stage in my life, I have more patience with the unsanitary newcomer who occasionally gets depressed and drunk than the sanitized charter member who regularly gossips, lies, cheats, and treats his family like dirt.

Stamped indelibly on my mind is the image of the elderly deacon who went ballistic over the fact that he drove by our church parking lot and witnessed teen-aged girls playing volleyball in slacks. Having tolerated his criticism in too many previous "bored" meetings, my cup "ranneth over", and I expressed my opinion that the scene of the volleyball game certainly would have been more appealing to the deacon, had the girls been jumping in their skirts.

I thought for a moment that possibly I should repent for my attitude toward this pharisaical behavior. Then I recalled the words of a famous Jewish leader who addressed this attitude two thousand years ago, when He called the religious leaders "white-washed sepulchers, full of dead men's bones....who would cross the sea to gain one convert, only to make him twice the son of hell." Thank you Jesus! I feel better!

CHANGING SEATS AND TESTING FRIENDSHIPS

Without a doubt, one of the most painful stages of transition is that of removing close friends or associates from their positions in the church. Some of these individuals will be charter members who sacrificed time, money, and energy to help bring the church to its current position. However, the vision and mission of the church often outgrows programs and staff members we started with. And when this happens, we simply cannot sacrifice our mission for the sake of programs, relationships, or positions that no longer propel us toward our goals.

Back in the late Seventies, while pastoring in Southern California, I invited Sherli Morgan to move from Texas and join our pastoral staff as our Minister of Music. As an accomplished musician, singer, and instructor, I knew Sherli had the ability to take our music department to a higher level, both musically and spiritually. And she didn't disappoint us. Sherli brought new life to our choir and orchestra, developed small singing groups, and directed outstanding seasonal productions for our children and adults. Everyone loved Sherli and her ability to bring the best of those she worked with. However, as time went by, I saw a potential ministry in Sherli that neither she, nor others around her had noticed.

One day during our staff meeting, I proposed to Sherli that she resign from the Music Department and become our Director of Children's Ministries. I shared with her my observations of her abilities and her potential with children, and told her I would give her a week to think and pray about it, but I felt very strongly we should make this transition.

At our next staff meeting, Sherli announced that she was reluctant to leave the Music Department, but was willing to make the move if I felt she should. My excitement and anticipation was high as we immediately began to make plans for Sherli to take the Children's Ministry to a new level. But my excitement and anticipation quickly turned to frustration from the moment Sherli announced her resignation at the next choir rehearsal. You would have thought we had announced I was closing the church and donating the property to Rev. Moon's Unification Church.

The following week was filled with non-stop phone calls and outrageous rumors that I had fired or demoted Sherli. There were even rumors of a "choir mutiny" in protest of my unwise and unjust decision. By the end of the first week, I was so sick of the crazy rumors and obvious distrust, I was seriously tempted to call Rev. Moon!

To say that Sherli's move to Children's Ministry was a good idea would be a tremendous understatement. For, not only did she transform our Children's Department, she went on to become a widely acclaimed voice for creativity in Children's Ministry and today, oversees a Children's Ministry several times larger than 85% of the churches across the United States.

For our congregation in California, for Sherli Morgan, and for the thousands of children who have grown up to be born-again Christian parents, the progress has been worth all the pain of criticism, distrust, and murmurings we endured. Thank God our ministry and our congregation survived the transition when Sherli changed seats on our bus. But what if Sherli had been on the wrong bus entirely? Now that's a horse of a different color! That's where the fur hits the fan! And if you are not very careful as a leader, that is where numbers of your people will suddenly "feel led" to go elsewhere!

If your church is more than five years old, and you have grown beyond the "family" stage, it is quite probable that your church has outgrown some of the departments and the leaders you started with. When you first started, you were quite happy to have Grandma Jones overseeing the Children's Ministry with her flannel graphs and six children attending. Back then, we were all just a happy little family ministering to those who chose to ride our bus. However, as the church has grown and the times have changed, we are now required by law to screen all our children's workers, to provide a safe, sanitary and secure environment for children. And the computer-savvy, techno children who attend require more than flannel graphs and Granny's rendition of "Father Abraham." You know changes have to be made if you are to maintain momentum and growth. However, not only is Grandma Jones a charter member

129

and faithful worker, she is also the mother of Deacon Jones! Not only are these scenarios real, they are really difficult.

I'm sure I shall never forget being called to lead a 75 year old church, with a membership well over five hundred and an antiquated bookkeeping system operating out a hand-written ledger. To complicate matters more, the office secretary/bookkeeper was a wonderful, gracious, kind, genuinely "born-again" grandma in her eighties.

Fortunately for me, the church board agreed it was time to computerize the church financial records, but unfortunately for me, this would jeopardize the present job of our resident office matriarch. Fortunately for me, I had what I considered a good relationship with the secretary, but unfortunately for me, it seemed she was related to half the congregation. Fortunately for me, with the help of a good CPA, we were able to convert the financial records to computer. But unfortunately for me, the CPA discovered a $25,000 discrepancy in the books.

Somehow, over the previous twenty-five to thirty years, mistakes had been made in the ledger that created a major miscalculation. Fortunately for me, the CPA conducted an audit, discovered, and corrected the mistake. But unfortunately for me, a few of my distracters seized upon the opportunity to accuse me of embezzling $25,000. Ouch, that was painful! However, that is just one of the prices we pay for being a pastor and working one day per week. In fact, whenever anyone remarks to me they wish they could be a pastor, and live such a leisurely and tranquil life, I always encourage them to go for it! However, as the first stage of pastoral preparation, I recommend that they receive permission to hang out with their pastor for one seven-day period; accompany him to the meetings with other pastors; go with him to the Chamber of Commerce meeting; sit in on his lunch meeting with the Mayor and Chief of Police...Oh, and during that seven-day period, answer all his phone calls 24/7; crawl out of bed in the wee hours of the morning and accompany him to the ER to stand beside the young parents whose child has just died from a ruptured appendix; even go with him to minister to the stranded motorist, who unable to reach the Salvation Army at 2AM on Sunday, somehow found the pastor's number and needs money for fuel to reach their dying grandmother in another state. (Be sure and take note of this scenario, for you will be absolutely amazed how many grandmothers in distant cities, die after midnight, on weekends, long after the Salvation Army and Rescue Missions have closed for the day) I usually inform the "aspiring wannabe-pastor" if he still wants to pursue full-time pastoral ministry after that seven-day period, come back to me and I will do all I can to assist him on his road to a life of leisure.

We survived the secretarial and bookkeeping transition by publicly honoring our veteran secretary with a fifty-year plaque, a floral bouquet, and lots of hugs and kisses. Obviously, transition does not come easily, but no organism can grow without it. Unfortunately for me, I had to pay the price of progress by making the hard choices to bring the church's financial records out of the dark ages. But fortunately for the pastor who eventually followed me, one major hurdle had been removed for him, and the church had progressed to a higher level of efficiency and integrity.

Well, that's my story, and I'm sticking to it! How about yours, Steve?

STEVE'S TAKE ON TRANSITION

After twelve years in my role as the Senior Pastor of the Journey in Russellville, Arkansas, we faced yet another crossroad of plateau and progress. We had grown from one to three weekend meetings; classrooms, nurseries and parking lots were all maxed out. And to further complicate matters, we had over 100 people driving 25-40 miles at a time when fuel prices had gone through the roof. We knew we had some difficult decisions to make if we were to move forward. The thought of launching another campus was exciting. But little did we know the emotional and relational stress we would experience to move to the next level. I thought that renovating a building multiple times over the past twelve years had been stressful enough, and facing the decision to transition my high-school buddy/best friend/hunting partner/staff member who was operating outside his calling and gifting was an experience I never wanted to repeat. But now I was facing an even more difficult decision.

131

In addition to the financial sacrifices required to launch the new campus, we were required to re-evaluate all ministry positions and responsibilities to ensure we were all operating at maximum efficiency. Adding the new campus caused us to rethink our ministry philosophies and procedures, and what we discovered was unsettling to say the least. For no longer were we responsible for ministry to one congregation in one location. Where once a department leader could concentrate his/her efforts on a single group, now it was becoming necessary to discover, disciple, and develop new leaders to facilitate the multi-campus vision.

Literally, our leaders had to become "Leaders of Leaders" and "Pastors of Pastors." In theory, this was an exciting and lofty idea! But in reality, it was an extremely painful transition. One of our ministry leaders had been on our pastoral staff for more than twenty years, first with my dad, and now with me, and without a doubt, was one of the most gifted, faithful, and dedicated servant-leaders I have ever known. However, when I shared with him he would have to transition from a local pastor to a pastor of pastors, it was more than he could handle. He thrived on studying the Word, researching, writing curriculum and music, and delivering his message each week at the local campus. Now, for the sake of our vision, I was asking him to do something he felt was completely beyond his calling, gifting, or desire. I asked him to pray about it and at least try it for the next ninety days. However, he came back to me a few weeks later and informed me he felt he was not the man for the job.

Can any of you out there pronounce Di-lem-ma? Here we had a close friend, a twenty-year veteran in our ministry, loved and admired by every family in our church, who said he could not do what we were requiring of him to move us to the next level. And to add complexity to paradoxity, our close friend and brother had a medical condition that could only be covered under our group plan. What to do? For the sake of avoiding rumors, confusion, and disunity, should we give him a fictitious title and provide him a permanent income in spite of the fact that he and we both knew the church had grown beyond his ability, or desire to function? Our decision was made for us when our beloved staff member met with our staff and delivered his decision to resign his position and trust

God for His leading to the next phase of ministry for his life and his family.

My personal response was a mixture of relief, combined with great concern for my friend and some anxiety over how this transition would be interpreted and received by our church family. In response to his resignation, we agreed to continue his salary for a period of ninety days to provide him with opportunity to seek God and secure employment elsewhere. At this writing, our gifted friend is working with another organization and, via the Internet, is expanding his outreach to churches across America through his creativity in musical productions.

If you are currently a church leader reading this book and you have not yet faced these heart-rending and potentially church-splitting decisions, your day is coming! And when the day arrives, you will be forced to make decisions that may alter your relationships between close friends and family members. At that crossroads, you'll decide to remain where you are and settle for status quo and redundancy, or you will make the hard choices to pay the price of progress and move forward. And when you do, if your decisions are balanced with love and compassion, yet commitment to God's Mission and Vision for His Church, you'll discover He is faithful to lead, to guide, and to provide for all who will continue to trust His will and His ways.

QUOTABLE QUOTES:

"It is hard to escape the conclusion that today one of the greatest roadblocks to the gospel of Jesus Christ is the institutional church" Howard Snyder (Howard A Snyder: Radical Renewal – The Problem of Wineskins Today - Touch Publications Houston, Texas 1996)

"The church is the church only when it exists for others." Dietrich Bonhoeffer (Bonhoeffer's Letters and Papers from Prison (Ed. Eberhard Bethge, New York: The Macmillan Company, 1972).

In a recent Church Leader blog, Greg Laurie reported: In a recent survey of 1,000 church attendees, respondents were asked, "Why does the church exist?" According to 89 percent, the church's purpose was "to take care of my family's and my spiritual needs." Only 11 percent said the purpose of the church is "to win the world for Jesus Christ."

These attitudes concern me and many other observers deeply. A business-driven response may only make things worse. In the long run, if we train consumers instead of communers, we'll end up with customers instead of disciples.

It might fill up an auditorium, but it will never turn the world upside down for Christ.

CHAPTER TWENTY ONE

Avoiding a Redundant Life

Recently a man sat in my office with a net worth of approximately one and a half million dollars. In addition to his multiple real estate holdings, his collection of antique and classic cars, and other valuable investments, this gentleman seemed to have everything required to make one happy. However, as I inquired about his well-being, his reply was "My greatest regret is waking up every morning." As I sat and listened, I immediately recalled the words of Solomon who wrote three thousand years ago, that money does not bring happiness. I also recalled the words of Jesus Christ who asked "What has a person profited who gains the whole world but loses his own soul?"

As I approach the end of this book, it has caused me to reflect on my own life. It seems just yesterday that I was leaving home for college. Imprinted on my mind is the image of my dad and mom standing in the front yard of our modest home in Bloomburg, Texas, watching me cut the strings and drive away toward my destiny.

As the youngest of three siblings, I was the last to leave home, with no understanding of the empty nest syndrome I was creating for Carrol and Rachel Pyle. Now, as I recall that moment, I realize more than ever why my dad brushed away tears that August morning in 1965. For my parents, it was the end of an era. A life season had ended and a new one had begun that would lead them toward their final earthly season.

At eighteen years old, I couldn't comprehend the scope of what was unfolding that morning. But now as I look back, I can more clearly see the bigger picture. As I turned away and aimed my car toward Waxahachie, Texas, the sun was rising for me and setting for my parents. Twenty three years later, my mother would be in heaven and my dad would be facing a lonely life in a nursing home. Georgiann and I would have three children of our own and would be nearing our own empty nest syndrome.

How did time pass so quickly? How is it possible that the color of my hair has turned from dark brown to salt and pepper to solid white? Even harder to comprehend is the fact that I have two sons with streaks of gray in their hair, and our youngest son now is the senior pastor of the church we pioneered two decades ago.

Today, again in my memory, I see my mother waving that tear-stained white handkerchief as I drive away into my future, and I realize I'm now holding the handkerchief. For Georgiann and me, the college days are history, and our children have children who will soon have children. And soon we will all make that final departure. When that day comes, I want to face it with the memory of a plaque my mom posted on a wall of our living room when I was a child. On the plaque was this message: "Only one life, twill soon be past. Only what's done for Christ will last."

It's really not that difficult if we live our lives with eternity in mind. Recently, I heard the story of a very wealthy man who died of cardiac arrest. At his funeral, one man said to another, "No one knows exactly how much he was worth. I wonder what he left behind." The other man replied, "Everything!" We will ALL leave it behind. In fact, all we will take to the other side is what we have invested in the Kingdom of God and eternal souls. No wonder Jesus admonished, "Don't lay up treasures here where moths and rust corrupt, or thieves break in and steal, but lay up treasures in heaven..." I believe the admonition for all of us is to find a place to serve others in each season of our lives, and do what we can, where we can, while we can!

I do not want my life to conclude like that of the wealthy man who sat in my office, whose greatest regret was waking that day. The challenge is before us all today, not to live a life of redundancy. So I issue this final challenge to each reader: Are you on the treadmill of life, just marking time, working, worrying and paying taxes? Or is your life counting for eternity? If you are still breathing, it is not too late to change direction. I challenge you to pay the price for true progress, break the curse of redundancy, and go for the ultimate prize of hearing our Heavenly Father say, "Well done, faithful servant, come on home!" If you not have prepared your heart and life to meet God, I urge to pray the following prayer as you close this book:

Father in Heaven, thank you for loving me so much you gave your only Son to purchase my salvation. Thank you for loving me in spite of my rebellious nature and behavior. Right now I repent of my sin and invite you to change my life. Come into my life and fill me with your presence. From this day forward I want to live for you and be prepared for the day you call me from this life into the next. Until then, please keep me pliable in your hands. Cause me to constantly be aware of the needs of others around me and cause me to seek out ways to meet those needs. And cause me to live my daily life with eternity in mind. Thank you for hearing me and thank you for saving me in the name of Jesus.

SUMMARY: There is ample evidence that the largest and fastest-growing evangelical churches in North America today were launched by leaders and a small group of individuals with a common goal of reaching the unconverted. Their rapid growth is largely due to their distinct advantage of limited religious baggage and traditional trappings. Most of these church leaders started with little or no money, equipment, or permanent facilities. They struggled through the challenges of pre-dawn set-ups in rented facilities, along with limited parking and child-care space. However, they lacked another element that propelled them quickly to numerical and spiritual growth. They lacked the burden of dealing with boards, bureaucrats, and Pharisees determined to maintain their status quo.

Many of you who have read this book may not have the opportunity, the time, nor the calling to pioneer a new work. Some of you find yourselves caught in the trap of religious redundancy and dead traditions. Others of you have been elected or appointed to shepherd a group of tired, sleepy saints just content to still be breathing and attending your meetings. (This group needs TLC too!) However, others of you cannot, and will not, be content to maintain status quo. You love those inside the fold, but your heart burns for those not yet rescued. It is to you the message of this book is directed. My prayer for you is the courage to make the necessary changes, the patience to endure the criticism of the religious crowd, and the passion of the heart of Christ to bring in the harvest ready for reaping.

If you feel you are ready and willing to accept this challenge, let me encourage you to begin with the following:

1. Spend seven days in prayer and fasting for God's plan for your ministry.

2. Identify the culture surrounding you and ask God how to connect with that culture.

ONE FINAL WORD:

In an earlier section, I emphasized that it takes much more than changing the name of your church to transition to an outreach church. With that in mind, let me issue one final caution. Let none of us think that bigger is always better. It is certainly true that living things grow. But let us all beware of the conclusion that we have become successful just because our buildings are full several times per weekend. Let us also remember that without the anointing of the Holy Spirit, our 22-minute contemporary praise and worship sets can become as redundant as the ritualistic singing of Eighteenth Century hymns. Finally, may we all be reminded that, in God's sight, a few persecuted believers gathered in an underground church in a Third-World country may well be more mature and progressive for the Kingdom than we.

The bottom line is this: We may attract crowds with our coffee, cappuccino, fog machines and light shows; we may capture and captivate great audiences with our talented musicians and vocalists. But it takes the power of the Holy Spirit to bring about spiritual conversion. And that power may not be found in the latest podcast or publication, but in the presence of, and communion with the King of Kings and Lord of Lords.

As a church leader, I place high value on the publications of cutting-edge leaders who are effectively spreading the Gospel. However, I am keenly aware that I must personally hear God's voice and display his nature and anointing to be effective where I live and minister.

I challenge each of you to prayerfully weigh the eternal rewards of God's mission and mandate against the temporal comforts of retirement and redundancy!

NOTES

1. The Victorian Society, No 26, Nov. 2007, www.victoriansociety.org.uk/publications/redundant-churches-who-cares/.

2. Ibid

3. Wikipedia: French Institute of Public Opinion

4. Enrichment Magazine, General Council of the Assemblies of God, pgs 31-32

5. U.S. News & World Report (July 26, 1989)

6. Ibid

7. Proverbs 14:12

8. Relevant Magazine, April 16, 2002, Relevant Media Group, Winter Park, FL

9. Ibid

10. Matthew 9:12

11. Amos 5:21-24 (The Message)

12. Isaiah 1:10-17 (The Message)

13. Matthew 6:7 (NIV)

14. Shannon O'Dell: Transforming the Rurals (Arkansas, Green Leaf Press, 2009)

15. I know I misspelled the word, but can't help but wonder if it was inspired!

16. Shannon O'Dell: Transforming the Rurals (Arkansas, Green Leaf Press, 2009)

17. Lisa Bevere: Lioness Arising (The Doubleday Religious Publishing Group) 2011

18. Warren Litzman: Jesus, Lost in the church (Treasure House) 1987

19. Steve Sjogren: Seeing Beyond Church Walls (Group Publishing,Inc.) 2001

20. Bill Hybels: Courageous Leadership (Grand Rapids, Zondervan) 2002

21. Ibid

22. Steve Sjogren: Seeing Beyond Church Walls (Group Publishing, Inc.) 2001

Made in the USA
Charleston, SC
09 January 2014